FLORIDA
GARDENING
MONTH BY MONTH

FLORIDA GARDENING MONTH BY MONTH

by Nixon Smiley

UNIVERSITY OF MIAMI PRESS
Coral Gables, Florida

Designed by Bernard Lipsky and Mary Lipson

Manufactured in the United States of America

Contents

Illustrations *7*

Foreword by Marjory Stoneman Douglas *9*

People and Gardens *15*

January First Signs of Florida Spring *25*

February Florida is Unforgettable *39*

March Dry, Windy, and Spring *53*

April A Month of Few Showers *63*

May First Month of the Rainy Season *77*

June First Month of Summer *93*

July Look for Comfort *107*

August Time for Armchair Gardening *119*

September A New Season Begins *135*

October End of the Rainy Season *149*

November Best Time of the Year *161*

December A Month of Color *173*

Bibliography *183*

Index *185*

Illustrations

Avocado varieties: Linda and Lula *28*
Floribunda roses *34*
The papaya as an ornamental *37*
Spanish bayonet *47*
Amaryllis *50*
Rooting softwood cuttings *55*
Bauhinia variegata, "the poor man's orchid tree" *59*
Landscape plan for a South Florida home *64*
Common weeds: pennywort and sandspurs *73*
Pruning diagram and instructions *81*
Air layering instructions and diagram *83*
Common pests: chinch bug, saddleback
   caterpillar, and lubber grasshopper *89*
Japanese beetle *90*
Orchids in an outdoor setting *102*
Lychees in South Florida *103*
Zebrina as a ground cover *114*
View of Fairchild Tropical Garden *122*
Japanese Garden on Watson Island *123*
Palms of three types *127*

Paurotis palms in a cluster   *128*
Black spot on rose leaves   *131*
Armyworm   *138*
Florida fern caterpillar   *138*
Spider mite   *144*
Millipede   *144*
Mole cricket   *159*
Cutworm   *159*
Aphid   *164*
Flower thrip   *178*
Thrip   *178*
Giant ficus tree   *178*

Foreword

That the small region of South Florida is unique in the entire continent of North America is an idea that thousands of residents, as well as floods of newcomers, often take years to understand. Its uniqueness is apparent at once in its climate; more slowly, perhaps, in the rare and wonderful nature of its plant material, by now a bewildering horticultural mixture of native and introduced tropic plant varieties and species. People have been forced to learn that gardening here, if not approached with an understanding of these unique conditions and materials, is doomed to failure.

It is only a short time, comparatively speaking, since botanists themselves began to recognize the plant possibilities of this region. Dr. Henry Perrine, whose career as a plant introducer in South Florida was cut short by his murder by Indians in the Seminole war of the last century, was the first to be impressed, and to impress the Congress of the United States, with the value of South Florida for growing introduced tropical plants. It was much later, in the 1900s, that Dr. John K. Small of the New York Botanical Garden began the region's first plant exploration, from Lake Okeechobee to the Florida Keys. Already before that time,

Dr. Henry Nehrling, the great plantsman of the lower west coast, and Dr. John C. Gifford, a nationally known forester on the lower east coast, had begun to make widely successful plant and tree introductions, at the same time advocating research to increase knowledge about native plants. Dr. Gifford left his mark on the Miami community as an author, teacher, civic leader, and public speaker.

Then, too, Professor Charles Torrey Simpson, fellow of the Smithsonian Institution, was developing his fine garden in Little River and writing, with the full magnetism of his great personality, books about the Florida wilderness that have since become classics. And Dr. David Fairchild, chief plant explorer for the U.S. Department of Agriculture, was more successful than anyone else in introducing rare and valuable plants and trees from the tropics. His work resulted in the establishment of the Fairchild Tropical Garden, the only botanical garden of its kind on the continent of North America, a garden now known and valued by many of the botanists of the world.

All of this accumulation of knowledge by scientists in the area needed interpretation in simpler and more popular form to become more effectively available to the general public. The readable and interesting small books by Mabel Dorn, whose frontier struggles to make a garden worked in her a passion for learning about plants and how to grow them in South Florida, were based on her close association and work with both Dr. Gifford and Dr. Fairchild. As founder of the area's first garden club and instigator of some fourteen others in the county, she brought about a great increase of interest and knowledge in gardening.

Of the other people who have followed these pioneers in knowledge and in practice, no one has been more widely known and followed, day by day, than Nixon Smiley. His years of experience as a garden editor, with his writings put to test in his own garden, and his association with scientists as director of the Fairchild Tropical Garden, have brought him the increasing attention of residents and newcomers alike—people whose eyes have been opened to the horticultural wealth of South Florida and whose desires have been kindled to grow gardens of their own, no matter how limited.

This revised edition of one of Nixon Smiley's most successful and valuable books comes, in a new, improved, and up-to-date form, as an answer to the demands of hundreds of would-be or experienced gardeners. Against the curious ignorance of many city dwellers who do not see the importance of keeping a green world around us, our air pure, and ourselves healthier and happier than would be possible on a peninsula of bare cement, this book arms us with a ready and valiant weapon.

Marjory Stoneman Douglas
October, 1970

FLORIDA
GARDENING
MONTH BY MONTH

People and Gardens

South Florida is internationally known as a garden spot for tropical plants. Each year increasing numbers of newcomers enthusiastically join resident gardeners in tending the soil of the only tropical region in the continental United States. These new residents, even if they have gardened extensively in different types of areas, are beginners in tropical gardening. Despite this fact, these newcomers are eager to start the gardening adventure that awaits them.

In few other places, even in the deep tropics, are there more kinds of ornamental plants—trees, palms, shrubs, and vines—from which to choose. For more than half a century tropical plants have been arriving in a constant flow from throughout the world's tropical zones to be planted and tested in the southern part of this lean peninsula. Since its establishment at the turn of the century, the United States Department of Agriculture's Plant Introduction Station at Miami's former Chapman Field has recorded in its accession book more than 14,000 tropical plants. Other tropical plants have been introduced by the University of Florida's Subtropical Experiment Station at Homestead, Fairchild Tropical Garden, nurserymen, and inspired amateurs. One amateur, Stuart publisher Edwin A. Menninger, took up plant introduction as a hobby and has introduced more than 800 flowering trees to Florida.

How many plants have been introduced to Florida and how many of these have survived is anybody's guess. Probably more than 20,000 kinds of plants have been introduced, from ground covers to giant banyans. If 5,000 have survived, it would take you nearly two years to learn their names if you were to memorize ten names a day. No one knows the names of all the introduced plants in South Florida or can identify most of them on sight.

Florida itself is the native home for an unusual collection of tropical trees and plants whose attractive bearing and hardy virtues are winning more gardeners to their culture. Best known among these and widely planted are the sea grape, the silver buttonwood, and the slender thrinax palm from the Florida Keys. South Florida is also the home of the handsome and versatile coco plum. Contrary to popular belief, it is not the home of the coconut palm. The coconut is only one of several trees and plants that have become so successfully naturalized here that they are considered state trademarks. Oranges and related citrus and the avocado are among other plants in this category. Also, the rich green grass lawns covering Florida have spread from imported turf. Saint Augustine grass comes from the West Indies, centipede from China, and zoysia from the Philippines and Japan. The rapidly expanding Florida house plant industry is also thriving on foreign transplants that find the state hospitable. The number of these successful introductions added to Florida's native plants indicates the unusual landscaping possibilities in this state.

Hazards Have Advantages

South Florida has some gardening hazards. Yet, strangely,

some of the things we call hazards are necessary aids to both ornamental gardening and to agriculture. For instance, we complain that we get too much rain in summer and not enough rain in winter. We would be better off, we say, if our fifty-five to sixty inches of annual rainfall were more evenly distributed over the twelve months. But would we? Isn't a dry season necessary for the best mango and lychee production? Isn't it true that many of the tropical flowering trees, shrubs, and vines make a poor showing in tropical areas where it rains all year? In such countries the mango may grow rapidly and make a huge tree, but it may bear few if any fruits. The most colorful bougainvilleas, poincianas, and cassias are found in parts of the world where the year is divided between wet and dry seasons, as in the Central American highlands. Florida would not have a $250,000,000 winter vegetable industry if its winters were rainy, for the best vegetables are grown during cool, dry weather.

Now consider another hazard, frost. Tender plants are occasionally nipped in South Florida when the thermometer dips into the lower thirties. Once in fifteen or twenty years we get a hard freeze all the way to downtown Miami. But is the cold really a hazard? If we had summer weather throughout the twelve months there would be no citrus industry, because cool weather is needed to sweeten our oranges and grapefruit. Citrus is not strictly a tropical plant; it is a temperate zone fruit, at home in that borderline area that separates the cold belt of the world from the hot. In the deep tropics citrus does well only in higher altitudes, between 3,500 and 5,500 feet. In the low, hot tropical areas citrus does not color up well, and its flavor may be flat, the fruit lacking in sugar and acid. Without cool weather, South Florida gardeners would have to abandon the idea of growing winter annuals.

Any newcomer to South Florida who attempts to garden

without first obtaining information about the peculiar problems of this area may quickly become discouraged. This does happen. A person who was a good gardener or farmer in a northern area may think he can be a successful gardener in South Florida by following the methods he used in a cooler climate. Hopefully, before he becomes too disgusted with gardening in Florida, he will learn that successful gardening in the tropics or subtropics requires new planting approaches.

In South Florida you work in your yard all year. The growth of some plants may slow down in winter and your lawn won't need mowing as often as in summer, but few things go completely dormant during the coolest part of the year. In every season, in every month, some plants are in bloom. In fact, we have more color in winter than during the warm, wet summer when plants are in lush growth.

Gardening has its Basic Rules

By learning and applying a few fundamental rules, however, anyone can become a topnotch gardener in South Florida. Proof of this is given by the evergreen lawns, lush shrubbery, colorful trees, and abundance of tropical fruit in fine gardens maintained by gardeners who had to learn from scratch. The basic rules for good gardening are simple and easy to apply. Here they are:

1. Plant acid-loving material in rich acid soil; plant those preferring a high pH in fertilized alkaline soil. (You can make the poorest soil rich by using fertilizers applied to the ground and to the leaves.)

2. Use planting material suitable for your soil or location. (Don't plant roses on the windswept seashore or avocados in the damp glades.)

3. Fertilize and water plants properly. (Find out how often you should water and fertilize your plants, make

notes of their schedules, and follow them. Too much and too little are common causes of plant problems.)

4. Keep plants free of insects and diseases. (Use preventive measures if possible. Begin control methods immediately after discovery of plant pests or disease. The longer you wait, the more time-consuming and expensive the process will be.)

Farmers and grove owners have to observe these rules in order to stay in business. You will have to observe them if you hope to be a topnotch plantsman. It is not necessary to bring in loads of black topsoil in order to grow good shrubs and trees. If your "soil" is nothing but sand or a mixture of sand and limestone rock, here's what you can do to grow a successful plant: dig a hole somewhat larger than you need for the roots of the plant, piling the soil to one side. Now incorporate into this pile of soil a heaping handful of sheep manure and enough peat moss so that you will have the equivalent of about one part of peat for every five or six parts of soil. Return some of this mixture to your planting hole. Set out your plant and shovel in the rest of the soil. You should have some soil left over. Use it to make a basin about the plant for holding water. Dust some dry fertilizer over the basin, just enough to whiten the soil a little, and fill the basin with water.

A newly set out plant should be soaked daily for the first couple of weeks, then watered daily every other day for awhile. After a plant is thoroughly established, weekly watering or watering every two or three weeks may be enough. Don't let light summer rains fool you into thinking that they provide enough water for your new plants. Irrigate whether it rains or not unless the rainfall equals an inch or more.

If you want to push young plants into rapid growth, fertilize them once a month for the first year. After plants have their growth you can cut down on the number of applications. Fertilize mature plants just enough to keep them in good health. If the leaves of tropical plants begin to turn a sickly yellow something is wrong. If you are sure that you are using enough fertilizer to keep them green, then try another trick. Spray the foliage with a minor element spray containing iron, manganese, and zinc. If a shrub or tree refuses to grow no matter how much fertilizer, water, and spray you use, maybe the best thing to do is to yank the plant out of the ground and replace it with another. If the plant is rare or one to which you have some sentimental attachment, there is another trick worth trying.

Dig up the plant and trim back its top. Then give the roots a good pruning, cutting off any that are twisted. Set the plant in a container of good soil, put it in shade, and water it daily. Feed it twice a week with a soluble fertilizer, mixed no stronger than recommended on the manufacturer's label. After two or three weeks, gradually wean the plant from the shade and get it used to the sun. After the first flush of new growth has hardened, reset the plant in a permanent location. Keep it fertilized and watered, and it should grow rapidly.

A plant may refuse to grow because it is too close to other trees or shrubs. Some plants are able to withstand competition better than others. Few plants of any kind can be expected to grow rapidly among pines, except perhaps leguminous species such as the native lysiloma or the woman's tongue tree. Rubber trees will grow among pines all right once they get established, but they are slow to get started.

Palms, especially the large species such as the coconut and royal, offer tremendous competition to other plants set close to them. You should not expect a hibiscus or a rose to do well at the base of a coconut. You may get some growth by watering and feeding, but in the long run the palm is bound to win.

To keep some plants looking their best you may have to give them extra attention. Before you add such plants to your yard, be sure you want to invest a little more time in their care. The ixora is one example of a shrub that may call for more maintenance. It is subject to attacks by aphids, scale, caterpillars, leaf-cutting wasps, sooty mold, and nutritional diseases. Furthermore, it does best in a soil that is slightly acid, while in Dade County the soil is more likely to be strongly alkaline and seldom neutral or acid in reaction.

The hibiscus likes soil similar to the ixora—slightly acid or neutral. It is also subject to yellowing in alkaline soil. Acid-loving plants such as these can be encouraged to do better in soil with a low pH by using an acid type of fertilizer or adding chelated iron to the ground. Despite these measures, many plants refuse to respond to reconditioning of the soil, among them camellias and gardenias. Gardenias in South Florida must be grafted on the related *Gardenia thunbergia* for success. The azalea is less demanding but requires some time to become established for best blooming.

To make insect and disease control take up less of your gardening time, keep alert for possible trouble and treat potential problems when they first appear. A heavy infestation of scale insects, for instance, may require several applications of spray before they are under control. If you let spider mites get ahead of you, you can do little but resolve not to let it happen again. These tiny pests arrive on leaves during the dry season, suck the juices from them, and cause the leaves to become rusty in color before they eventually drop. Dusting occasionally with sulphur or spraying with some other miticide from November until spring will put an end to the spider mite problem. This and other pest and disease problems will be discussed at length elsewhere in this book.

Always Buy the Best

Rule Number 5 urges the gardener to select the best plants available. If the plant is tagged with the FNGA Gold Seal, this is easy. The seal guarantees that the plant is at least graded Number 1 by the Grades and Standards section of the Florida Department of Agriculture's Division of Plant Industry. That means that only the show-graded Florida Fancy is better, and this grade is not necessary for ordinary home landscaping use.

If the nursery you visit, however, does not identify its plants by the Gold Seal, a voluntary identification program, you can learn to spot the best purchase yourself. Look around the nursery and check the condition of the plants and their containers. Do the plants look healthy, or do many of them resemble the gnarled, dwarfed plants that the Japanese take a hundred years to grow? Are the containers rusty or partially decayed? If so, chances are that this nurseryman has a poor turnover and he may also be a poor grower. You cannot even be sure his plants are the varieties they are represented to be. After plants have been in a nursery for several years, their tags may become lost or confused. Buying from a well-known nursery will help remove these hazards.

Here's another tip: don't make your plant selections from northern seed company catalogs or magazine ads without first checking to see if the product will thrive in South Florida. With the exception of certain annuals planted at the right season, few will. You can feel certain that a giant flowering violet tree from upper New York State or a fall-blooming ice plant from Labrador will not grow in our tropical climate.

Few of the northern bulb favorites will do well in this area. Some gardeners here, however, go to great lengths to get tulips to flower, buying the bulbs in the fall, storing them in the refrigerator until January, taking them out and planting them, and then throwing them out after they flower.

In general, it is best to buy plants locally from nursery-men who are acquainted with your soil and climate and can advise you on maintenance of materials that look well year round.

Month-by-Month Guide

Now that you have been introduced to South Florida gardening, its problems and possibilities, you are invited to take a close look at practical Florida gardening month by month, with notes on temperatures and reminders of seasonal chores. To locate information on any one subject as it appears throughout the months, consult the index.

JANUARY

First Signs of Florida Spring

January, a cold month in the North, is the first month of "spring" in South Florida. Don't look at the calendar though. You won't find spring there until March twenty-first, nor will you find it in downtown Miami or in a swank Miami Beach hotel. No, you've got to get out into the glades and cypress swamps to see evidences of an early spring—to see the bald cypress and the scrub willow coming out in bright new growth, or the live oaks in the hammocks loaded with yellowish catkin flowers. If you go deep into the boggy swamps of the Big Cypress, you may see the southern maples sending out their reddish new leaves in January.

It's quite a sight to visit Big Cypress Swamp between January and March, with the strands of green cypress or the pine and cabbage palm hammocks standing out against a foreground prairie of winter-killed glade grasses, colored here and there with the bright bloom of wild flowers.

Vast Wild Area Being Preserved

South Florida is an unusual country, a country where a unique civilization is being built along the border of one of the wildest areas left in the United States. Along a narrow strip of coastline extending from West Palm Beach to Homestead, an amazing population growth is taking place. This area is roughly seventy-five miles long and ten to twenty miles in width. On the east side is the Atlantic Ocean and on the west is the Everglades, a wild expanse of sawgrass that has for half a century resisted taming in spite of man's expenditure of vast quantities of energy, imagination, and money. During the first quarter of this century the Everglades were drained. The result was not a Garden of Eden as reclaimers had visualized but despoliation. In 1948 Congress approved a plan drawn up by the Army Corps of Engineers to correct the mistakes of the early developers. This plan, which will cost nearly one-half billion dollars by the time it is completed, has been severely criticized by conservationists, who contend the Corps of Engineers destroys more of the wilderness than it preserves. The sharpest criticism against the Corps has been in connection with the Everglades National Park, whose glades and sloughs in times past received an uninterrupted flow of water from the north. Now that flow of water is controlled by levees and spillways built by the Corps of Engineers. In defense of the Corps, its plan was made many years before the biological research was done that revealed the subtle ecological links in nature that man so often upsets by his reclamations, developments, and improvements. Harkening to the criticism of its vast Everglades flood control works and their operations, the Corps has attempted to correct the weaknesses of the original plan that sought to provide protection against both floods and droughts for over 20,000 square miles in southeast Florida. Meanwhile, the Everglades National Park has by no means been destroyed. Although its wildlife may never return in the abundance of its earlier days, there is still plenty to be seen by visitors to this vast wilderness at Miami's back door. The extensive wildlife and feeling of wilderness in the Everglades National Park make it one of the greatest parks in our country.

Dade's Citrus is Persian Lime

January is a good month to see the citrus groves of central Florida. By the middle of the month over 800,000 acres of orange, grapefruit, and tangerine trees color the landscape with their orange-yellow fruits. Highways take you through the middle of groves, and you see the orange and deep green of row after row of heavily-fruited citrus trees on either side. These winding roads and colorful groves make an unforgettable picture.

Many people visiting Miami for the first time expect to see large citrus groves on the outskirts of the city. Southeast Florida, however, is not citrus country. At least, it's not an important place for oranges, grapefruits, and tangerines. There is a thriving Persian lime industry in Dade County, though, with more than 4,000 acres planted in groves. The multimillion dollar citrus industry, where most of the frozen concentrate is packed and the great bulk of Florida's citrus fruit is grown, is in central Florida. Other important citrus groves lie along Indian River, where the famous "Indian River fruit" is produced. Because of its high eating quality, most of the fruit goes into the fresh fruit market.

Citrus is not the only fruit that matures in January. Several avocado varieties ripen this month, including the Choquette, Taylor, Linda, and Wagner. These fruits can be harvested as you need them, for they will hang on the trees for several weeks yet. Harvest the larger fruits first.

An Important Month for the Gardener

January is one of the most important months of the year for the tropical fruit grower and the South Florida gardener.

Avocados vary widely in appearance and flavor, from round and rough-skinned Linda (left) to the longer, smoother Lula.

What you do or don't do this month may be reflected in flower and fruit production over the next twelve months.

First of all, January is the month for fertilizing fruit trees, lawns, and shrubbery. You can't grow much fruit without feeding the trees that produce it, even where the soil is fairly rich. In South Florida, where the soil is notably poor, you must feed your fruit trees regularly and usually heavily. All tropical fruit trees except mangos should be fertilized in January. (Mangos, as you will learn in the December guide, should be fertilized when they begin to bloom, whether it is December, January, or February.)

To learn the type and amount of fertilizer you should apply, you may call the county agricultural agent's office for answers to specific questions or to request some of the many booklets available through that office. Some garden supply stores have salesmen who can tell you how many fifty-pound bags of fertilizer you need if you tell them first how large your lot is, how many fruit trees you have and what size they are, and how many other plants you intend to fertilize. You can also obtain bulletins from the Institute of Food and Agricultural Sciences at the University of Florida in Gainesville. Local newspapers are also good sources of information on plant care.

Learn How to Grow Good Citrus

It has been my experience that anyone who can grow good citrus in Florida can grow just about anything. There are few other plants in the world that are subject to more insect pests and plant diseases. I don't know of any other type of fruit tree that has more nutritional troubles than the citrus. Citrus is attacked by aphids, whitefly, bugs, caterpillars, grasshoppers, and various scale insects. Citrus is beset by sooty mold fungus, foot rot, gummosis, tristeza or quick-decline, melanose (which discolors the fruit), and "greasy spot" on leaves. Citrus may also suffer from deficiency diseases caused by insufficient zinc, copper, or magnesium.

No matter whether you are starting out with young citrus trees or have bought a place that contains several old citrus trees, January is a good month to start planning year-round care for your trees. Let's say that you have three orange trees, a Hamlin, a Temple, and a Valencia; a Marsh seedless grapefruit; a Minneola tangelo; a Dancy tangerine, and a key lime tree. The trees were planted three years ago and are now a little over head high. Distribute about three pounds of fertilizer around each tree, except for the lime. Give the lime tree only half the amount recommended for the others.

How do we arrive at these recommendations? Well, there's no way of working out a foolproof, scientific system for determining a tree's exact needs. By soil tests and leaf analysis it might be possible to approximate the kind and amount of fertilizer any tree needs; but this method would require a great deal of work and expense. For the homeowner, the thing to do is remember your citrus needs fertilizer and put it down. But how much? A rule of thumb calls for applying about one pound of fertilizer for each year of a citrus tree's age. This rule can also be applied rather roughly to any other tree that is expected to produce an annual crop of fruit for you. This rule of thumb is used by plant scientists, grove owners, and amateur horticulturists alike.

In suggesting such a rule of thumb method, it is assumed that the gardener will take certain things into consideration. For instance, he should realize that a three-year-old tree that is only a foot high—a tree that hasn't grown any since it was planted—doesn't need three pounds of fertilizer. The reason for putting three pounds of fertilizer around a three-year-old orange tree and only a pound and a half around a three-year-old key lime tree is that the key lime tree does better when kept slightly on the "hungry side." If your key lime tree has reached good size, is bearing well, and looks good, it may need only one or two applications of fertilizer a year, whereas it is customary to fertilize other kinds of citrus, including Persian limes, three times a year, in January, May or June, and again after the middle of October. A key lime tree that is overfertilized and pushed into rapid, lush growth most of the year becomes susceptible to a fungus disease that kills the new twigs.

When fertilizing citrus, or any other kind of plant for that matter, do not pile the fertilizer around the trunk but scatter it well over the ground beneath the branches and a little beyond.

Fertilizer Shorthand Not Difficult

When you buy a bag of fertilizer in Florida, you will find a tag listing the plant foods in the fertilizer and their percentages. When your garden supply store man recommends that you apply a "6-6-6 fertilizer," he is using a kind of shorthand. A 6-6-6 fertilizer is a mixture containing 6 percent nitrogen, 6 percent phosphate, and 6 percent potash. This order of listing ingredients is invariable. A 6-6-6 is considered a general purpose fertilizer. When you buy a hundred-pound bag of such fertilizer, you get eighteen pounds of plant foods and eighty-two pounds of "filler." "What's this filler for?" you may ask. And why are you having to pay for eight-two pounds "of nothing"? That fertilizer tag will do much to answer your questions. You will notice that the 6 percent nitrogen is derived from two sources, chemical and organic. The chemical nitrogen may come from nitrate nitrogen and ammoniacal nitrogen, while the organic nitrogen may be derived from castor pumace, dried blood, tankage, fish scraps, and the like. These organic nitrogen sources make up the eighty-two pounds of "filler." Most of the chemical nitrogen is readily available to plants as soon as it goes into solution, but the organic nitrogen must first be broken down chemically in the soil, becoming available to plant roots little by little. The more organic nitrogen there is in the filler, the more you have to pay for a bag of fertilizer, because organic nitrogen is more expensive than chemical nitrogen. In winter you can use the cheaper chemical nitrogen fertilizers, while in the summer you should use the more expensive organic fertilizers. Why? The heavy summer rains wash the chemical nitrogen through the soil and beyond the reach of the roots. The organic nitrogen, however, is released slowly over a period of several weeks or months.

We have said very little about the action of fertilizer. Nor will we go very far into this subject, since it is tough enough for a scientist of the Ph.D. level. There are a few things that you should know about these elements called plant food. You perhaps already know from school science courses that plants require more than a dozen elements—most of them in extremely small amounts. These elements include such minerals as copper, zinc, manganese, boron, and iron. Soils usually contain these elements in such sufficient quantity that none has to be added to fertilizer. In Florida soils, however, these minerals may be in the soil in such small amounts that plants growing in the soil become sickly, refuse to grow, and eventually die from malnutrition. On the other hand, these minor elements may be plentiful but tied up in insoluble compounds and not available to plant roots. Iron is one of the best examples of such an element. With pounds of iron about the roots, plants can suffer from iron deficiency, their leaves yellowing, if the iron is in an insoluble state. If humus is supplied to the soil in the form of mulch, the acid released by the decaying leaves, grass clippings, and similar materials will act on the compounds containing iron, and thus small amounts of iron will be released in a soluble, free state, to be absorbed by plant roots. Bacteria and fungi go to work on the mulch and other organic material, breaking it down with their complicated chemistry and thus releasing tiny amounts of other needed elements, such as zinc, copper, and manganese. The decaying organic material also releases other elements, including nitrogen, phosphorus, and potash. Ordinary mulching materials do not contain these elements in sufficient amounts to supply the needs of growing and fruiting plants in Florida. While mulching should be practiced, it is necessary to supplement the chemicals released by the mulch with regular applications of commercial fertilizer. Citrus and many other sensitive plants may not get enough of the minor elements from the soil or even from decaying organic matter to supply their needs. For that reason it is a good idea to apply a nutritional spray to citrus once a year.

Apply Nutritional Spray This Month

Commercial citrus growers apply nutritional spray in

January—a practice recommended by the Citrus Experiment Station at Lake Alfred. Every garden store in South Florida probably carries materials for nutritional spray: copper, zinc, manganese, and iron. These elements are usually packaged together, with recommendations for mixing solutions on the label. Until recent years it was necessary to add lime in order to neutralize the chemicals used. Otherwise severe burning of leaves could result. But chemical companies have come out with "neutral metals" that do not burn (when used in recommended amounts) and do not form insoluble compounds with other metals in the soil. They are, however, absorbed by plant leaves and plant stems. Since these metals may stain severely, do not get them on painted surfaces or on sidewalks or driveways. Add a detergent or another kind of spreader so that the solution will form a film over the leaves of your trees. Otherwise, the solution will form large droplets on the surface of waxy leaves, and much of it will be lost as the droplets are shed by the leaves.

The fertilizer and nutritional spray treatment recommended for citrus can be repeated for avocados, lychees, guavas, West Indian cherries, sapodillas, and even for such heavy flowering plants as hibiscus, ixoras, and allamandas.

Spring Beds Are Planned Now

January is the time to plan and plant the spring vegetable and flower garden. Get beds made and seeds or plants in the ground before the end of the month. On the farm, growers in the Immokalee area will be planting watermelons; in fact, many farmers planted acres of watermelons even in December, hoping to come in with the first carload of melons for the northern market while snow is still on the ground up there.

January is usually so dry that you can expect to spend a good deal of time irrigating your lawn. It becomes increasingly harder to keep lawns green. An application of fertilizer

Regular dusting and the selection of hardy plants such as these floribundas make rose growing successful in South Florida.

may help if water fails to "green up" the grass. But if you fertilized centipede grass in the fall, better be careful about putting more fertilizer on it. Try spraying centipede first with neutral iron or with iron sulphate mixed at the rate of a level tablespoonful per gallon of water. Don't get this staining material on sidewalks or walls. If the iron doesn't help the centipede, try feeding the centipede with not more than fifteen pounds of fertilizer per 1,000 square feet. Always irrigate well the day before fertilizing and irrigate lightly afterward to wash the fertilizer off grass leaves and into the soil.

Rose bushes should be blooming prolifically by the middle of January if you have treated them right. Dust the plants weekly with a rose dust containing sulphur and insecticides. When watering roses do not let the sprinkler play on the plants, but let the water run freely from a hose over the rose beds. Do not walk through your rose bushes while the plants are wet from dew or rain. This suggestion also applies to your annual beds and vegetable garden. Many a gardener transports fungus diseases from one plant to another.

January Weather Calendar

Following are the average temperature, rainfall, and wind velocity figures for a normal January in the Miami area. The figures are based on official weather bureau records. This is no forecast, but the information presented may provide you with enough weather facts to picture an average January in Miami.

Temperature. Average daily high: 75.5; average daily low: 58.3. Highest temperature ever recorded for the month: 87 in 1947; lowest temperature: 28 in 1939.

Rainfall. Average: 2.18 inches. Wettest January: 7.93 inches in 1926. Driest January: .04 of an inch in 1951.

Wind. Prevailing direction from the north-northwest. Average velocity: 9.4 miles an hour. Highest wind ever recorded during the month in Miami: 50 miles an hour in 1940.

Hurricanes. No hurricane has ever hit Florida in January.

Frost. Protection needed during the month.

January Planting Calendar

Vegetables. Beans, beets, broccoli, Brussels sprouts, cabbage cantaloupe, carrots, cauliflower, collards, cucumbers, eggplants, endive, garden peas, kale, kohlrabi, lettuce, mustard, onion sets, parsley, peppers, potatoes, pumpkins, radishes, romaine, rutabagas, spinach, squash, sweet corn, Swiss chard, tomatoes, turnips, and watermelons.

Flowers. Asters, baby's breath, bachelor's buttons, balsam, calendulas, candytuft, carnations, cosmos, cockscomb, daisies, forget-me-nots, gaillardia, globe amaranth, hollyhocks, lace flowers, larkspur, lobelias, lupins, marigolds, morning glories, nasturtiums, pansies, periwinkles, petunias, phlox, pinks, poppies, portulacas, salvia, scabiosa, snapdragons, statice, stock, strawflowers, sweet peas, sweet william, and verbenas.

Bulbs. Amaryllis, caladiums, callas, cannas, dahlias, gladiolus, iris, lilies, narcissus, tuberoses, and zephyranthes.

January Garden Guide

Fertilizing. Feed fruit trees and shrubbery this month.

Nutritional spray. Apply spray containing copper, zinc, manganese, and iron to fruit trees and to shrubs subject to nutritional deficiencies. Get no spray on walls or on walks.

Watering. Much needed this month. Put down the equivalent of one inch or more of rain at each irrigation.

Insects. Plant mites will begin to get bad this month. Dust susceptible plants, especially citrus and avocados, with sulphur every two months.

Spring garden. Get annuals and vegetables planted this month for spring garden.

Papayas. This is a good month to plant papaya seeds. The idea is to get plants ready for planting in permanent locations by the time warm growing weather rolls around. It takes about forty-five days to raise a papaya plant to transplant size of five to seven inches. But after a papaya plant is set in the ground and pushed with fertilizer, it will make a big, six- or seven-foot plant by fall and bear large quantities of fruit.

An exotic looking fruit with an unusual taste, the papaya makes a striking ornamental tree. It likes to be well watered and fertilized.

FEBRUARY

Florida is Unforgettable

February is very much like January. The temperature and rainfall are about the same for both months. Both months are comparatively dry. Skies are clear and bright blue except for scattered cottony clouds, and the sun is comfortably warm. The nights are usually cool.

The clear skies and bright sun of January and February have made South Florida a fabulous winter vacation land. It is an unforgettable experience to get off a plane at Miami's International Airport, little over two hours' flying time from the snowbound North, and step out into the bright, drowsy sunshine. But the picture is not complete until the visitor has seen the area's miles of beaches, with thousands of vacationers seeking the bone-warming sun. You can often guess how long a visitor has been here by the color of his skin—whether it is white, pink, or burned. If he has been here long enough to have a deep tan, then perhaps he is a winter resident. One thing is sure: he's not a native. Natives and permanent residents seldom go to the beach during the winter, preferring to go when the weather is warmer.

Plants More Sensitive Than Humans

While February is very much like January, spring will be just around the corner by the time this short month is over. Although the change will be imperceptible to man, the thermometer will be on its way upward. Maybe people won't notice the difference, but plants and birds will.

Watermelon vines, which grow rather slowly during cool weather, will be "taking off" by the time the end of February rolls around. Unless a disastrous freeze hits South Florida farms, the first ripe watermelons of the season will begin moving northward before the end of March. February is a big month for other winter vegetables. Tomatoes and potatoes by the truckload will be moving northward from Dade County daily. Other truckloads of vegetables will go out from markets at Belle Glade and Pompano and from Florida's west coast. Conscientious home gardeners check the calendar and figure it's getting high time to put in a spring garden if they intend to plant one this year.

In February most of the migratory birds begin returning to Florida for the flight back to northern nesting grounds. These are the birds that "jumped off" from the Florida peninsula last fall, winging across the Caribbean to spend the winter in the more tropical lands of the West Indies and in Central and South America. The migratory birds won't be wearing properly visaed passports about their necks. But one day you'll notice an increase in the number of new birds at your feeding station, if you maintain one.

You may say to yourself, "Why, these birds came through here only a few weeks ago, it seems, on their way southward. Now they're already back. How come?"

Birds have as many idiosyncracies as people. Take the swallows, for instance. They begin arriving in South Florida in August from northern nesting grounds. They must have left their northern homes a month before, flying southward in easy stages, feeding over fields and meadows on the way.

They hang around South Florida for several weeks, doing their graceful acrobatics over glades and vegetable fields as they feed "on the wing." Then they take off, southward, some of them going as far as Brazil. Before February is over they're on their way back north, arriving in Florida in sizable numbers. The first contingent often arrives as early as January.

The swallows reach their northern nesting grounds only after the ground has thawed and the temperature is warm enough for them to survive and to begin the annual job of nest building. As soon as the young are raised and put on their own, the older birds head south again. People who know birds say the older birds leave the breeding grounds a few weeks ahead of their offspring. The young birds follow after they have become adept at long flight. How they find their way along the same route followed by the parent birds has for years been the subject of scientific study.

How To Attract Birds

Many people won't set up feeding stations on their property for fear of attracting an overabundance of noisy sparrows and raucous bluejays. But there is another way to attract birds. Plant lots of cover for them—especially fruit-producing cover. Many shrubs and small trees yield fruit that both birds and humans can enjoy. As good a bird fruit as you will find is the Barbados cherry *(Malpighia glabra)*. The fruit of this bush, known also as the West Indian cherry or acerola, has been called a living vitamin pill because it contains so much vitamin C, around 100 milligrams of vitamin C per cherry. The Barbados cherry yields several crops during the spring and summer. To get a good variety it is best to buy an air-layered plant from a nurseryman. Get a couple of varieties, both sweet and sour. Birds like the fruit a great deal. If there is a covey of quail in the area, they may visit a Barbados cherry tree almost daily while it is in fruit, eating the cherries that drop to the ground.

Another good bird tree is the fast growing muntinga, a small tree that almost constantly produces scarlet berry-like fruits. Woodpeckers really go for muntingas, visiting the trees several times a day to fill up on the fruits. Other plants that yield bird-attracting fruits are the governor's plum, ardisia, guava, severenia, and duranta. And no tree is better than an oak for attracting the little birds, such as the warblers, that like to walk up and down the rough bark in search of tiny insects. Some of the leguminous trees, such as the native lysiloma, also attract small birds, because their small leaflets harbor very tiny insects the birds like. These bird-attracting plants can be used in landscaping just as well as a hibiscus or a banyan.

This Is Last Big Month for Planting

February is the final month in which the planting calendar is wide open for both vegetables and annuals. Even so, hot weather may catch many plants seeded now before they reach producing size. For this reason it is better to set out plants this month that were seeded in January or late December. February is late for planting sweet corn unless, like a full-fledged farmer, you are prepared to spray weekly with a fungicide to prevent corn blight. But if you are among those who like to try your hand at growing watermelons, February is a good time to plant.

Watermelons need about ninety-five days to reach maturity under normal growing conditions. Melons planted in December or early in January may take longer. Florida soils are much too poor to produce melons without the use of large quantities of fertilizer. Back in the days when every farm had its horses and mules, farmers used to put a bushel or more of stable manure in each watermelon hill. Since high quality animal compost is hard to obtain any more, farmers now use commercial fertilizers altogether.

Here's a suggestion on growing melons: Plant eight feet apart, in rows and in hills. In each planting site mix a heaping double handful of peat moss and a heaping handful of a garden type of fertilizer with the soil to a depth of eight inches. Soak the soil thoroughly with water. A week later plant six watermelon seeds in each hill about one inch deep. Don't drop all the seeds in one hole but scatter them out over an area of several square inches. After the plants develop their first true leaves, thin out the weaker plants, leaving no more than three plants in each hill. Make a second fertilizer application, a heaping handful, as the plants begin to run. Scatter the fertilizer over an area of a foot or eighteen inches about the hills and irrigate lightly to wash the fertilizer into the soil. Fertilize a third time when you see the first bloom. Never get any fertilizer on the foliage of your plants or close enough to the main stems to risk burning the roots. The fast growing roots travel far and wide. You can apply fertilizer as far away as three feet after the vines have spread out five or six feet in all directions. And how would you apply fertilizer without getting it on the vines after they have covered the ground for several feet about each hill? Simply lift the vines very carefully from one side and lay them over on the other side of the row. Dig three shallow trenches at distances of eighteen inches, two feet, and thirty inches from each hill. Put fertilizer in these trenches and cover it. Replace the vines. Now lift the vines from the other side of the row and apply fertilizer in the same manner. After the first watermelons have formed, do not try to turn the vines.

Watermelons are subject to insects and diseases. For this reason it is a good idea to spray the plants weekly with a solution of wettable lindane and zineb, mixed according to the manufacturer's directions. If you cannot find wettable lindane and zineb at garden stores, you can buy them from a farm supply store. You should never apply any kind of insecticide that contains oil to melon vines or to vegetables.

Think about Spring Color Now

If you don't care to be bothered with growing annuals for spring color, plant a few beds of caladiums now. If planted in February, caladium tubers will do well on either the west or the east side of the house. If you make rich beds for the plants and keep them well watered, you can even plant caladiums in full sun this month. Just plan to water them daily or every other day.

Mix some peat moss with the soil at planting time, and don't let anybody tell you that caladiums don't need fertilizer because "plenty of food is stored in the tubers." While caladiums will grow without fertilizer, starved plants won't reach full development. The fertilizer required to produce a bed of fine caladiums costs only a few pennies. At planting time, some growers mix fresh sphagnum moss with the tubers and also scatter half an inch or so of sphagnum over the beds to serve as a mulch. After the plants begin to develop mature leaves, dust them once a month with sulphur to ward off a possible infestation of red spider or other plant mites. Where caladiums are planted in limestone soil, feed them with an acid fertilizer, much as is used for gardenias.

If you want beds of annuals for spring bloom, read the suggestions for making beds in the September and October calendars. It is possible to purchase a wide variety of plants from seed stores or from nurserymen. In fact, beginning gardeners may be wise to buy their plants from professional growers, who usually know which varieties do well in South Florida and which do not.

Citrus Quality Is Tops Now

One of Florida's best months for citrus is February, when the Valencia oranges ripen. If you've been getting your citrus out of six-ounce cans, you've probably forgotten how a good orange tastes. There is no better way to remember than with the tender pulp of a nearly seedless Valencia.

Both January and February are ideal months to visit central Florida, where the highway winds through orange groves for miles on end and where you see truck after truck loaded with colorful oranges on their way to concentrate plants. For most of Florida's oranges now go into cans for the frozen juice market.

If your own backyard citrus trees are not producing good fruit, something is wrong. Maybe you have not fertilized properly, maybe you haven't applied a nutritional spray periodically, or maybe you've watered too much. If you really want good citrus, follow the recommendations for citrus culture listed in the January guide.

Keeping the Landscape Green

Since everything is so dry at this time of year, it's a good idea to be extremely careful with fire. A cigarette or match carelessly tossed along a roadside may start a fire that will sweep through hundreds of acres. No thinking, conscientious person will toss lighted cigarettes or pieces of paper or other litter from a car. The cigarette is dangerous, and the litter takes the edge off the beauty of parkways and woods. A large percentage of our forest fires, however, are caused by careless cigarette smokers, and nowhere are parkways any more badly littered than in South Florida, despite efforts to get visitors and residents not to be "litterbugs."

To keep lawns green and to prevent many shrubs and trees from shedding their leaves, you'll need to do a great deal of watering. Newcomers to the tropics may think it quite odd for tropical trees to shed their leaves. In many places of the tropical world, however, the seasons are sharply divided into wet and dry. During the wet season everything is green, but after the dry season has been underway for five or six months, a great many of the trees have dropped their leaves. The same will happen in South Florida unless plants are watered.

Some plants do not show marked changes in appearance from one month to the other all year. The pines do shed, but they never become bare of leaves. They remain green all year. No palm is deciduous (losing all of its leaves periodically), although palms may suffer during drought, especially when transplanted during the previous summer or fall. During long dry spells palmettos and cabbage palms may become dry enough to become fire hazards, but their leaves do not turn yellow and drop, as do the leaves of many trees. Palmetto leaves, which contain large quantities of wax, make a terrifically hot fire when they become ignited.

Drought-Resistant Plants

Among the drought-resistant shrubs none is more outstanding than the native coco plum, which seems to thrive in dry land as well as in wet land, once it becomes well established. This plant takes pruning well, and its evergreen leaves are handsome all year. It is easily propagated by seed. Its slow growing habit makes it popular with gardeners who dislike pruning and want a compact plant for a particular landscaping need.

The Spanish bayonet or yucca is a natural for those seeking drought-resistant plants. Groups of Spanish bayonet plants always lend themselves well to landscaping the so-called ranch-style houses, because of the association, perhaps. Since it can withstand a constant spray of salt and sand, Spanish bayonet does well on the seashore. While cacti

The dramatic Spanish bayonet resists salt spray and drought.

do well without water, the desert varieties don't usually thrive in South Florida, finding our climate too moist much of the year. We do have a native opuntia, or prickly pear cactus, which does well even when planted in containers and neglected for months on end. It has a very handsome yellow bloom.

Is Fertilizing in Winter Bad?

Does it injure tropical plants to fertilize them in winter? Obviously I don't think so, since I recommended fertilizing lawns, fruit trees, and shrubbery in January. Many people, however, believe that plants should be "hardened up" in the fall with potash and then fed no more until spring.

There is no evidence that a "potash-hardened" plant is capable of surviving a freeze any better than a plant that has received a balanced fertilizing containing not only potash but also the other elements such as nitrogen, phosphorous, and magnesium. The Subtropical Experiment Station at Homestead has found that an avocado that has received its normal fertilizer requirement has a better chance of surviving a freeze than a tree that has not been fertilized.

Plants with yellow leaves, deficient in minerals, seem to be much more susceptible to cold than plants whose leaves have a healthy green color and whose sap is loaded with minerals.

Periodic watering during extremely dry weather is also necessary, for without some moisture in the soil a plant cannot take up minerals through its roots, no matter how much fertilizer you apply. Remember, however, that it is easy to injure plants with fertilizer during dry weather. If you apply fertilizer to dry soil and then irrigate, plants will gorge themselves on the mineral-loaded water. Burning of roots and of leaves and stems may result. Water well one day and fertilize the next; then wash the fertilizer into the soil with a light irrigation. Your plants, their roots wet from the previous day's irrigation, will not be able to gorge themselves on minerals. Heavy applications of fertilizer in winter are usually unwarranted. Rather make applications light, and repeat when needed.

If you have any old run-down trees about your place, such as a large live oak, a gumbo limbo, or a gnarled sea grape, an application of fertilizer in February will help to bring them back to good health during the months ahead. Tree experts recommend the application of three pounds of fertilizer for each inch of a tree's diameter. Take the measurement four or five feet above the ground. A tree one foot in diameter needs thirty-six pounds of fertilizer. But don't spread all the fertilizer in a circle close to the trunk.

Spread it out under the tree as far out as the branches extend.

February Weather Calendar

Following are the average temperature, rainfall, and wind velocity figures for a normal February in the Miami area.

Temperature. Average daily high: 76.8; average daily low: 58.8 (Inland temperatures are three to four degrees warmer during the day and three to four degrees cooler at night.) Highest temperature ever recorded for the month: 89 in 1956: lowest temperature: 27 in 1917.

Rainfall. Average: 1.91 inches. Wettest February: 6.56 inches in 1956. Driest February: 1944; only a trace of rain fell during the month.

Wind. Prevailing direction from the east-southeast. Average velocity: 9.9 miles an hour. Highest wind ever recorded during the month of February: 41 miles an hour in 1947.

Hurricanes. No hurricane has ever hit Florida during any February on record.

Frost. Protection needed throughout the month. The lowest official temperature ever recorded in Miami was during the freeze of February 3, 1917, when the thermometer dipped to 27 and remained there most of the night. On the same night a low of 26 degrees was recorded at the United States Plant Introduction Garden, then located on Brickell Avenue.

February Planting Calendar

Vegetables. Beans, beets, broccoli, Brussels sprouts, cabbage, cantaloupe, carrots, cauliflower, collards, cucumbers, eggplants, endive, kale, leaf lettuce, mustard, parsley, peppers, pumpkins, radishes, romaine, spinach, squash, sweet corn, Swiss chard, tomatoes, turnips, and watermelons.

Flowers. Asters, baby's breath, bachelor's buttons, balsam, calendulas, candytuft, carnations, cosmos, cockscomb, daisies, forget-me-nots, gaillardias, globe amaranth, hollyhocks, lace flowers, lobelias, lupins, marigolds, morning glories, nasturtiums, periwinkles, petunias, phlox, pinks, poppies, portulacas, salvia, scabiosa, snapdragons, statice, stock, strawflowers, sweet william, and verbenas.

Bulbs. Amaryllis, caladiums, callas, cannas, dahlias, gladiolus, iris, lilies, narcissus, tuberoses, and zephyranthes.

Amaryllis are bulbs that favor tropical conditions and can be left in the ground year round.

February Garden Chores

Watering. Many plants will begin to lose their leaves this month if they are not watered periodically. Weekly or twice-weekly watering of grass is sufficient if at least an inch of water is put down each time.

Propagation. This is a good month to make cuttings of many popular ornamentals such as ixora, hisbiscus, duranta, aralia, crotons, and jasmine. If you prefer to make new plants by air layering, wait until the first of April to begin propagations.

Poinsettias. Usually these plants will stay in bloom until March if they are healthy. You can cut them back this month and take cuttings if the plants have become straggly. For more information on poinsettias, see the March calendar.

Lawns. If you need a quick green lawn, it's not too late to seed rye. It will last until hot weather.

Insects. If you haven't done any dusting with sulphur this season, signs of mite infestation may begin to show up now. Such signs are rusty or faded leaves, perhaps with some leaf shedding. There will be more shedding in March and April if the mites are not brought under control. Dusting monthly with sulphur will give fair control of most mites.

Spring garden. You should have finished your final general planting in January. You can still plant a number of things, but it's better to buy started plants from a seed store or nursery.

MARCH

Dry, Windy, and Spring

If you're a new resident in South Florida, resist that spring urge this month. It's all right to thumb through those colorful seed catalogs, dreaming about the possibilities of duplicating the masterpieces of the "green thumbed" photographer who made the pictures. But if you want to be sure that you raise what you plant, better consider this reading for entertainment only.

While March may be the first month of spring throughout the northern hemisphere, it's not the month for starting "spring" gardens in South Florida. Sure, it's possible to plant a few vegetables and annuals this month and grow them to maturity. In fact, South Florida gardeners can grow vegetables and annuals the year round. But the planting calendar is no longer wide open: the time has passed when you could plant all the things you were used to growing in your garden in the North.

In South Florida we prepare our garden sites and flower beds in September and October, and plant in October and November. Planting can be continued periodically until February. March is getting late for most things, although some folks with greener thumbs than most of us are able to plant and grow many "borderline" fruits and vegetables this month. A short planting calendar at the end of this chapter lists the vegetables and annuals recommended for planting at this time. Compare it with the planting calendars for the months from September to February.

Be Prepared To Irrigate

If you insist on planting some of the crops recommended for March, better be prepared to provide irrigation and to fight insects. You can keep your garden out of insect trouble, at least most of the time, by spraying all plants weekly with a lindane-fungicide combination. Apply the mixture to your plants weekly with a pressure-type sprayer to keep down most insects and most diseases. If you wish, you can add a soluble fertilizer. Never apply insecticides in your garden during the morning while the plants are wet or while bees and wasps are at work among the flowers of such crops as beans or melons. Instead, make the application in the afternoon. One additional precaution if you intend to plant pole beans in your spring garden: Dust weekly with sulphur in addition to using the spray combination. The sulphur is necessary to control rust, a disease that the new fungicides do not control. Apply the combination spray and the dust at different times. Never apply insecticides to vegetables within a month of the time you expect to harvest them.

Prune Poinsettias This Month

Although it's 300 days till Christmas, March is the time to prepare for your next Yuletime color by giving your poinsettia plants the attention they demand. It's time to cut back plants that have been in bloom since December and to propagate new plants by rooting cuttings.

To root softwood cuttings, make a slanting cut through the stem two to six inches from the tip. Remove all but three or four leaves and insert the cutting to about half its length in the rooting medium. Keep moist and out of direct sun.

There is no certain date for cutting back poinsettias. You could have done it in February if your plants were ragged and the bloom faded. And if you still have good-looking plants in colorful bloom, don't prune them until the color fades or until you get tired of looking at poinsettia flowers.

Few plants are easier to root than poinsettias. Take cuttings about a foot long. Root them in clean sand, burying about five inches of the basal ends. Be careful that you don't get the cuttings upside down—they do better growing in the direction in which nature started them. Eight-inch clay pots make good containers for rooting poinsettias. You can root several sticks in a single pot. Roots form within a few weeks. The rooted cuttings can then be carefully shaken out of the container, separated, and planted in individual containers: or they can be planted in permanent locations in hedge rows, in beds, or along the house foundation.

Cuttings should be taken from healthy, vigorous plants—never from plants affected with poinsettia scab. This disease is caused by a fungus that gets beneath the bark and kills the cambial layer. It seems to be worse where plants are kept moist. When the disease becomes severe, it may succeed in girdling the stems of your poinsettia plants and killing them. Keeping the stems of affected plants painted with a solution of neutral copper may help them to overcome mild attacks of the disease. Make the solution by dissolving a tablespoonful of neutral copper in a pint of water.

There are some tricks in pruning poinsettias and in training the plants into bushy shrubs. They're good tricks to know, for you can use them in pruning and training other shrubs, and even vines.

How far back you should cut a poinsettia plant depends on the size and strength of the poinsettia plant itself. But never cut it back to the main stem. Say, for instance, you wish to prune a plant that has four branches growing out from the main stem. Cut them back to within six or eight inches of the main stem. If your plant is a rather large one and each of the four branches makes several smaller branches, you may simply cut back those outer branches to a length of six inches.

Train Plants into Busy Shrubs

At the time of pruning give your plants a shot of fertilizer and irrigate them well. Within a few weeks new growth will commence. If this growth is not a healthy deep green, something's wrong. Maybe you haven't given them enough fertilizer. If they are healthy, the new sprouts will grow rather rapidly. And here's where one of those little tricks we've been talking about comes in handy. After each bit of new growth gets to be about six inches long, pinch out the terminal bud at the tip end of the shoot. This will encourage additional branching. Within a few weeks you'll notice several new branches coming. And when each one of these new ones gets to be six inches long, remove the terminal bud from each of them.

Watch Out for Citrus Insects

Citrus will be bursting out in new growth and flowers this

month. Almost invariably the first new growth will be attacked by aphids that will curl the leaves and make them unsightly. Better keep some nicotine sulphate or malathion on hand to spray immediately after the first signs of new growth. You may need to repeat the application in a few days. Also be sure to remove all dead twigs from your citrus trees early this month if you haven't already done so.

March is still in the dry season. During this month and April you still have to worry about keeping lawns and plants irrigated. Furthermore, the weather begins warming up rapidly in March; and a combination of warm, dry weather and a constant southeast breeze dries out your plants before you realize it. Potted plants in nurseries must be watered almost every day. But a soaking of the soil once a week is usually enough for grass and shrubbery. That, however, depends on where your home is located. Your lawn and plants may need more water if you're living on a sandy ridge.

Since frost is still possible throughout most of South Florida, be prepared to protect small, tender plants. Miami has had a low temperature of thirty-four degrees during March, which is low enough for frost to form.

Don't Understimate the Value of Mulch

During the dry spring, mulch around plants pays big dividends. Its value for most soils in South Florida can't be overemphasized. Mulch does six things:

1. Preserves moisture in the soil.

2. Protects the soil from the intense heat of the sun.

3. Provides a constant supply of organic material.

4. Prevents the quick drying of the soil during the windy, dry period of late winter and early spring.

5. Gives some protection to susceptible plants against rootknot-causing nematodes.

6. Improves soil.

Any kind of organic material that is subject to decay within a reasonable time is good mulching material. You can use grass clippings, leaves, weeds, wood shavings, shredded coconut fiber straw, peat moss, or cane waste from sugar mills.

You can even use large limestone rocks—long used to advantage by old-timers in the Miami area and in the Florida Keys. Unless placed properly, however, the rocks can be unsightly. Also, they do not provide much protection against the growth of weeds. Peat moss is a practical mulching material. For special plants, especially young avocados or mangos, scatter a shovelful of shredded tree bark over the mulch. Everglades peat, known more commonly as muck, is not recommended as a mulching material.

Fallen leaves make a good mulch, and leaves bedded about trees and shrubbery may not be so bad to look at. Their brown color provides contrast to the green in your plants and grass.

Mulching provides some nutrients, but not enough for young plants or fruit trees. Use as much fertilizer on a young tree that you have mulched as on one that you haven't. When trees reach maturity, then you can adjust your fertilizing to suit the tree's needs. When a tree receives large quantities of mulch over a period of years, you'll find the organic content of the soil is high. The tree is then able to obtain much of its nutrients from the soil.

Florida Ushers in Spring

The nation's spring first appears in Florida. We may not notice spring so much in South Florida, where there are many kinds of trees, shrubs, and vines in bloom every month. But even here we perhaps have more things in bloom during March than in any other month. The bombax, which bloomed in January and February, is just about over blooming by March and is coming out in bright new growth.

But *Tabebuia argentea*, the silver trumpet tree, is in full bloom this month. And the callistemon or bottlebrush tree is in full show, its red flowers, shaped like bottle brushes, hanging in heavy clusters from the weeping branches. The spathodea is also in bloom, holding its heavy clusters of torch-colored flowers toward the sky. Many shrubs are also in bloom in March, and the bougainvilleas are still in good color. Showiest of all the locally grown bauhinias, the poor man's orchid tree, is in bloom throughout March. This tree covers itself with orchid-like flowers after shedding its leaves, thus making a spectacular show, especially along parkways and in parks where it is planted in masses. One of the showiest parkways in South Florida is along Old Cutler Road just north of Matheson Hammock, where large clumps of the *Bauhinia variegata* trees were planted several years ago by the Dade County Parks Department.

Not an orchid relative but a worthy rival, Bauhinia variegata, *"the poor man's orchid tree," is widely planted.*

In the northern part of Florida the temperate zone trees are in full bloom by the first of March, including the dogwood and redbud trees, the azaleas, and the wisteria, while the annuals are at their very best. Easter lilies also begin flowering all over the state, while the amaryllis is in bloom throughout the month.

This is also the month for a favorite plant of mine to bloom. It is the Okinawan hawthorne. While on Okinawa during World War II, I saw a slender, well-formed evergreen tree growing beside a Seabee-built road near Buckner Bay, not far from the village of Chimu. The tree, about 20 feet high, was in fruit but it was green. Fortunately I was able to collect ripe fruits from the tree some months later, and I sent the seed to Adolph C. Jordahn, who was then superintendent of the Robert H. Montgomery estate south of Miami.

When I returned home the plants were making good growth. Two plants that Mr. Jordahn planted on the Montgomery estate bore their first flowers in 1948. It was the first time I had seen the plant in bloom, since it was through blooming when I arrived at Okinawa in 1945. From a distance the blooms looked like apple blossoms.

I cut a specimen, including a twig with foliage and flowers intact, pressed it, and sent it to Dr. S. G. Blake of the division of plant exploration and introduction of the U.S. Department of Agriculture in Beltsville, Maryland. He identified it as *Raphiolepis indica*. A plant of this name, introduced to the United States several years ago, is described in L. H. Bailey's *Hortus Second* as a five-foot shrub, a native of South China. Seeds from the Okinawa raphiolepis, however, made six-foot plants in three years and eventually became small trees. While the Chinese and Okinawa raphiolepis are the same species of plants, they seem to be distinct varieties. The Okinawa raphiolepis has been distributed by the Fairchild Tropical Garden.

March Weather Calendar

Following are the average temperature, rainfall, and wind velocity figures for a normal March in Miami.

Temperature. Average daily high: 79.5; average daily low: 62.4. Highest temperature ever recorded for March: 90 in 1964; lowest temperature: 33 in 1940.

Rainfall. Average: 2.14 inches. Wettest March: 7.22 inches in 1949. Driest March: .02 of an inch in 1956.

Wind. Prevailing direction from the southeast. Average velocity: 10.2 miles an hour. Highest wind ever recorded during March in Miami: 53 miles an hour in 1936.

Hurricanes. There have been no hurricanes in Florida during the month of March.

Frost. Frost protection needed throughout most of the peninsula during March.

March Planting Calendar

Vegetables. Cantaloupe, collards, cowpeas, mustard, okra, papayas, peanuts, pole beans, pumpkins, New Zealand spinach, squash, sweet potatoes, turnips (for tops), and watermelons.

Flowers. Balsam, cosmos, cockscomb, forget-me-nots, gaillardias, petunias, phlox, portulacas, salvia, scabiosa, strawflowers, and zinnias.

Bulbs. Achimines, amaryllis, begonias, caladiums, gladioli, gloxinias, lilies, and zephyranthes.

March Garden Chores

Fires. March is a dry, windy month. Build no fires near woods or piles of trash where a spark may ignite a blaze. Palmettos and pine straw burn fiercely during this time of year. Even the dead grass along parkways may become ignited from cigarette butts carelessly tossed out. That's why it's a good idea to put out cigarette butts in automobile receptacles.

Bulbs. Both achimines and gloxinias can be started this month.

Insects. Keep up spraying or dusting for plant mites. They can cause defoliation of plants during the dry weather we normally have at this time of the year.

Propagation. If you need large numbers of hibiscus, aralias, crotons, and other plants for hedges, this is a good month to make cuttings.

APRIL

A Month of Few Showers

April showers may bring spring flowers in the North, but in South Florida April is usually a rather dry and windy month. If you want spring flowers, it's safer to depend on irrigation for the average rainfall for April is under three and a half inches. In some years less than an inch of rain may fall. The most rainfall recorded in Miami in any April during the first half of this century was 20.40 inches in 1942. It came down more like a flood than an April shower, though, with nine inches falling in a single day.

In April we begin to prepare for the summer. Because of habit, it may be difficult for many newcomers from the North to resist wholesale planting of beds of annuals. And those who planted spring vegetables in the North may want to make a garden here. Just as I said in the March calendar, you can grow a variety of vegetables and annuals in South Florida throughout the year, but it takes experience and a constancy that gardening in the North did not require. If you insist on trying a late spring or summer garden, better buy started plants from a nurseryman rather than attempt to grow them from seed.

Plan Your Summer Landscaping Program

Planting annuals now means waging an uphill battle against insects and diseases. Instead, why not spend your energy in planning landscaping improvements for your grounds? Maybe your foundation plants need renovating or transplanting. Maybe some trees are too close to the house and should be transplanted or removed if transplanting is not practical. Perhaps you want to plant some fruit trees

A successfully balanced garden composition is both restful to the eye and interesting. Here, trees, shrubs, and ground covers are planted in gradually curving beds that not only break the geometrical outlines of the property but make mowing easier. Low-growing plants are placed under windows for easy maintenance and an unobstructed view.

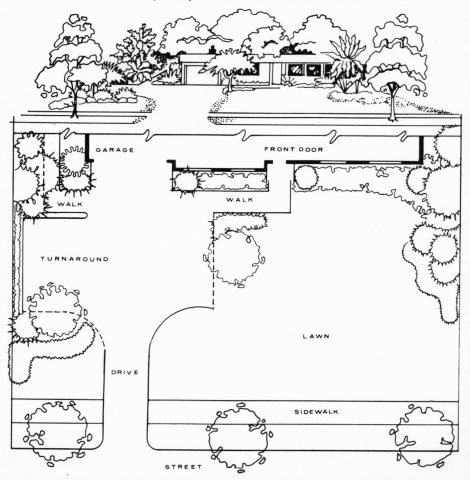

this year, say a couple of orange trees, a grapefruit tree, and an avocado. April is a good month for making overall plans. Make decisions this month and carry them out during the summer.

One of the easiest ways to improve your landscaping is to draw up a plan of your grounds, including your house and the existing plants. Do it to scale. This is easy. Buy a tablet of eight by ten inch graph paper, the kind engineers use. If you prefer a larger plan, buy sheets of graph paper as big as you like. It's very simple to draw to scale on this kind of paper. Indicate the placement of plants by drawing them lightly with a pencil. If there are several plants in the middle of the yard, try moving them about on the plan. Erase them from their present locations and place them near the borders. Clear out the middle completely and try to . visualize how your grounds would look if you made the changes.

Now if you intend to plant those fruit trees you've been wanting, plot them in near the borders and see how they would look. Consider your fruit trees not wholly as fruit producers but also as ornamentals. Don't line them up in rows, as you would in an orchard. When grown as ornamentals, they will produce just as much fruit as when lined up like soldiers.

Root Prune Now for Transplanting Later

If you intend to transplant shrubs or trees when the rainy season begins in June, April is a good month to root prune them. Root pruning will make transplanting very simple, greatly reducing the risks of losing your plants.

In order to root prune a plant you must first consider the size of the plant and estimate the size of the ball of earth and roots you hope to move with it. Then with grubbing hoe and shovel cut a trench around the plant. The size of the ball left in the middle will depend on the size of the shrub or tree. Make the trench the width of the shovel and a foot to eighteen inches deep. Fill the trench with leaves or other debris and let it stand for the next couple of months. The soil removed from the trench can be piled out of sight until you need it for refilling the hole after the plant is relocated.

Meanwhile, roots will grow in the ball of earth left about the plant. Be sure to water the plant regularly. Fertilize it lightly every two weeks or so to encourage the rapid development of roots within the ball. Once the ball of earth is full of roots, you can move the plant with little risk of losing it. First you will have the job of cutting the roots on the bottom of the ball. An old ax is ideal for this job, especially in rocky soil. Cut as far underneath the ball as you can and remove the soil with a shovel. Now tilt the tree first one way and then another, cutting the roots in the bottom-center of the ball. If you have no one to help you, a rope will do the job of holding the plant tilted to one side.

If your plant is too large to move in a wheelbarrow, or if the root ball is too bulky and heavy to ride along on a shovel or a wide board, you can make a sled for transporting it. Attach a cable or a chain to the sled and pull it with a car or truck. You will need help, since someone must hold the plant on the sled as it is being pulled along. Large trees weighing up to a thousand pounds can be transported short distances on a sled, if you do the job right. Root-pruned trees, incidentally, don't have to be cut back severely since the ball of roots will support nearly a full top. Cutting back about one-third of the top is usually sufficient.

Start Cuttings Now

This is a good month to begin rooting cuttings. For rooting difficult cuttings, such as *Gardenia thunbergia,* the wild African plant on which the cultivated gardenia is budded, here is a tip: Get a ten-inch clay pot and a pane of glass to cover it. Fill the pot to three-fourths full with fine or medium crushed granite (You can buy this material from feed supply stores if garden stores don't carry it.) Sink your cuttings in the granite, saturate with water, and cover with the pane of glass. Sprinkle daily to keep moist, and keep the cuttings under shade.

For cuttings, select twigs from healthy new growth. Cuttings taken from older plants are more difficult to make root than cuttings from young, vigorous plants. The wood of the cutting should be about half mature. Remove only the lower leaves from each cutting, keeping a rosette of leaves around the bud. Veteran gardeners will tell you that the best time to take cuttings is after the first flush of spring growth, just before the new wood has hardened up. If you know ahead of time that you will take cuttings from a certain plant, it's best to give it a shot of fertilizer in February or March and water it well to encourage a robust growth. Be sure to give the plant a good soaking the day before taking cuttings so that the tissue will be full of water.

Limestone Soil May Be the Best Soil

If you live in the rocky soil of south Dade County, don't be too quick to curse the soil and say you can't do a thing with it. Sure, a new place "on the rock" may be hard to work, but after you become its master, limestone soil is one of the most easily managed soils in Florida.

Although the soil of south Dade County is classified as "Rockdale soil," its character varies a great deal. Many of the rock ridges appear to be solid masses of bleached rock. Yet even in this apparently solid rock, pines, wild shrubs, and smaller plants grow in abundance. In other areas the rock is mixed with yellow sand; in a few others a layer of sand covers the rock to a depth of six or eight inches. Many homes are built on land-filled sites, particularly at Miami Beach, on bay islands, and along waterfronts onetime occupied by mangrove forests. In the 1960s developers began filling marl glades that were onetime prosperous tomato farms and creating subdivisions.

The native plant life varies a great deal, according to the elevation of the land and the character of the soil. Caribbean pines with a heavy understory of scrub palmetto are the conspicuous plants of the "high" rockland. Other important wild plants also grow in the south Dade pine-woods, including the summer flowering tetrazygia and the slender silver palm. Then there are the hammocks, where live oaks, strangler figs, mastic, gumbo limbo, lancewood, and the several kinds of eugenias live in a dense community that resembles the true tropical jungle. These dense plant communities, or hammocks, are believed to originate in areas that for one reason or another have escaped serious fire for a number of years. Once established, the hammocks do not burn readily, for the thickly growing trees shade out grasses and other annual plants that die in the fall, making the pinewoods like tinder during the winter dry season.

In all areas of the south Dade rock country there are "pot holes," where the sand is several feet deep. In these pot holes early settlers planted bananas and pineapples and raised their vegetables. They tried their hands at clearing the pineland and planting fruit trees, but the plantings were limited to the sand pockets in the rock. Dynamite eventually became widely used for making tree holes, but today it is seldom used. Before a grove is planted today, a farmer hires a land clearing outfit to push over the pines with a bulldozer. The pines and brush are piled up and burned. Then a "rock plow" is attached to the bulldozer, and the rockland is scarified to a depth of about six inches. The land is then "back-bladed" or leveled by the bulldozer, and planting stakes are set for the planting crew. Beneath this thin layer of rock and sand, euphemistically called soil, is an almost solid formation of white rock known by geologists as Miami oolite. Plant roots are confined to the top six inches of scarified soil—a fact you should bear in mind when caring for plants in such soil.

When freshly scarified, limestone soil is not the best soil in the world. It contains free lime that goes into solution when the soil is moist. The result is a highly alkaline soil, so alkaline that the few minerals are "tied up" in compounds, unavailable to the plants. Unless given the proper treatment, many plants sicken when planted in freshly scarified limestone. They develop deficiency diseases, their leaves turning yellow and the twigs dying back from lack of enough copper, manganese, or zinc. They may suffer severely from iron deficiency, the leaves turning a pale yellow, with only the leaf veins remaining green.

During their first year, plants set in limestone soil should be fertilized monthly and sprayed every three months with a solution containing copper, zinc, manganese, and iron. Mulching is important. Use grass, weeds, peat moss, or anything that will cover the soil and either decay rapidly or release acids in small amounts to aid in neutralizing the lime in the soil.

Humus Solves the Problem

It may surprise you to learn that many of the tropical hammock plants, which appear to be thriving in limestone soil, really prefer an acid soil. How, then, do they manage to grow so well in limestone? Here's what happens in a hammock: Leaf fall covers the limestone soil with an accumulation of decaying humus. With every rain a new supply of acid is carried into the soil, where it comes in contact with the surfaces of the limestone rock and into crevices containing plant roots. The acid not only opens ways for the roots but also neutralizes free lime and keeps the surface of limestone rock harmless as a source of alkaline "poisoning." The acid also helps to break down chemical compounds in the soil, releasing minute amounts of nutrient minerals to be absorbed by the eager, expanding roots.

You can approximate the same situation in your own yard by mulching and fertilizing. Under a large amount of mulch the surface of limestock rock eventually becomes covered with algae or bacterial growth, and the white, new appearance vanishes. The mellowing rock soil is now becoming a perfect place for your shrubs, trees, and palms. After fertilizing monthly for the first year, you can reduce the number of applications to three a year and apply nutritional spray only once a year.

Limestone soil holds moisture much longer than sandy soil. By irrigating established trees once every month you should be able to keep even the most thirsty varieties in top condition.

If you wish to leave the pines about your homesite, do not scarify among them with a heavy bulldozer. This practice, although widely followed, weakens your pines in two ways. With their main roots destroyed, the pines are easily toppled in a high wind. They also become susceptible to pinebark beetles, and once these beetles invade a pine, there is hardly a chance of saving the tree from almost certain death.

There is a way to clear the underbrush about pines without too much risk. Insist on the use of a light bulldozer rather than a heavy one. Don't pay any attention to a contractor who tells you his smart operator can use a heavy machine without plowing. It's difficult to avoid plowing into the rocky surface about pines with a heavy machine even when the operator tries.

A light machine does a somewhat messy job, but the roots of your trees won't be badly damaged. Furthermore, a small dozer can get into places that a larger machine can't enter without destroying trees.

If you intend to clear the underbrush and bring in marl as a topsoil, maybe it's just as well to bulldoze the pines in the first place. Pines usually live about fifteen years after a heavy layer of marl has been spread about their roots. To save your pines, use a sandy soil or even a rocky fill in preference to marl.

Whether to leave pines or take them out has to be decided from two viewpoints. If the site where you intend to build is a mass of exposed, jagged limestone rock, with very little sandy material mixed with it, clearing and scarifying prior to building may be the best thing to do. If this seems necessary, go ahead and clear the pines and burn them. If it is practical to do so, simply leave islands of pines, permitting the bulldozer to plow around the pines but not too closely and never in between them.

Begin Fighting Lawn Weeds Now

You may notice a rather odd thing taking place in the lawn during April. If it has been fertilized and kept well watered, the grass is beginning to come out of its wintertime lethargy, but the weeds are growing much faster than the grass. With this kind of uneven competition taking place, your lawn may be covered with weeds by the time summer is over. That, at least, is what you're likely to think.

Well, you can put those weeds in their place by spraying them with weed killer, but herbicides must be used with care and following professional recommendations. Different grasses and weeds call for different measures.

The presence of weeds is often a sign of inadequate lawn care. One of the "weed and feed" products on the market may be all you need to kill the weeds and strengthen your grass so that it can crowd out weed competition. If you are just starting a lawn, a pre-emergence herbicide should be applied a few days after you lay the lawn to prevent weed development.

All weed killers should be applied to small test areas first to determine the effect on the grass. Different grasses find different materials toxic so general recommendations can not be made.

If you have Saint Augustine grass, use weed killer in half the strength recommended for other grasses. Otherwise you may burn your grass or even kill it for Saint Augustine is more sensitive to weed killers than most other grasses. Rather than risk injuring your grass, be prepared to make three or four applications of a weak solution rather than one strong solution.

To understand the danger of using weed killers carelessly, you should know a little about them. There are several kinds, but they come under two primary headings—selective and nonselective weed killers. When used according to directions, a selective weed killer will kill certain plants and do no harm to others. The hormone type killer, 2, 4-D, kills broadleaf plants but does not injure grass. Use it for spot treatment only; don't broadcast. Another selective weed killer, Dowpon, will kill grasses but will not prove very damaging to broadleaved plants. The nonselective weed killers, such as CMU, sodium chlorate, and ammonium sulfamate, kill both broadleaf plants and grasses.

These weed killers are very potent. For instance, 2,4-D is active when diluted at the rate of one ounce of the chemical in 1,000,000 ounces of water. (One ounce in over 7,800 gallons.) When you know this, it's easy to understand why you have to be exact when mixing solutions. Weed killers also act on your ornamental plants, so apply the material only when there is no breeze. The weed killer will distort

Common weeds such as pennywort (left) and sandspurs can best be controlled by preventive measures.

the leaves of shrubs or trees and even ruin beds of annuals and some types of foliage plants, especially ground covers.

Weed killers must be absorbed by weeds in order to be effective. Once mixed with the plant's juices, the hormone is carried throughout the plant's tissues. It kills by disrupting the plant's internal chemical processes. That's why it may take several days before weeds begin showing signs of weakening. But don't expect a selective weed killer recommended for lawns to kill unwanted grasses. Your weed killer doesn't know the difference between a weed and a valuable plant. If your zoysia grass is overrun by Bermuda grass, don't expect a selective weed killer to kill the Bermuda just because you have branded it as a weed. And don't expect a selective weed killer to work wonders on nut grass. You can kill nut grass by continual use of weed killers, but it takes time. Although nut grass is not a true grass but a sedge, it is still resistant to weed killers.

Many Trees Change Foliage This Month

South Florida, from January to May, seems to be in perpetual spring. The bright yellow-green leaves of the mahoganies and black olives (bucida) give the Miami area an atmosphere of spring through part of March and April. Another tree that is striking in its new foliage is the pongam, which is being widely planted as a hurricane-resistant tree. Along about the first of March the pongam begins to throw off its old foliage. Then, as soon as the branches are bare and the reddish-brown leaves lie on the ground, the pongam begins to put on its bright new growth. These trees are so striking in new growth that they seem to be in bloom.

Another tree that puts on new foliage immediately after shedding the old is the sacred fig of India. Its aspen-like leaves hang on until April, when they all seem to turn loose almost at once and go spinning to the ground. A deep pile of the yellow-brown leaves collects under a big tree. But before you know it, the tree is fully leaved again, with new heart-shaped leaves that seem to swivel on long stems, catching the light and flashing it into your eyes.

Not all trees replace their foliage immediately after shedding. The woman's tongue tree is bare of foliage for several weeks in the spring. These trees present an unusual sight, clothed only in their dry seedpods, which clatter in the wind and remind some of a group of talkative women.

The poinciana, which sheds its foliage a little at a time, is nearly bare of leaves by the time its blooming season arrives in June. There are exceptions. Occasionally you'll find a poinciana that doesn't shed its leaves completely. These "evergreen" poincianas, however, do not seem to be very good flowering trees.

April brings much color to Florida. The daylilies are in full bloom this month, and the annual beds planted back in January and February are masses of color now. The blue jacaranda trees are also in flower at this time.

April, though seldom too cold, is the last month of the so-called cool season. May is usually pleasant, but it is not nearly so cool as April. April is more like November than it is like any other month. All and all, April is one of South Florida's most pleasant months, and I always hate to see it pass.

April Weather Calendar

Following are the average temperature, rainfall, and wind velocity figures for a normal April in the Miami area.

Temperature. The weather warms rapidly this month. The average daily high is 82.6, compared with 76.8 in February. The average daily low is 66.6, compared with 58.8 in February.

Rainfall. Average: 3.51 inches. Wettest April: 20.42 inches in 1942. Driest April: .15 inches in 1967.

Wind. Prevailing direction from the east-southeast. Average velocity: 10.4 miles an hour. Highest wind ever recorded during April in Miami: 70 miles an hour in 1950.

Hurricanes. There have been no hurricanes in Florida during April.

April Planting Calendar

Vegetables. Cantaloupe, collards, cowpeas, mustard, papayas, okra, peanuts, pumpkins, New Zealand spinach, squash, turnips, and watermelons.

Flowers. Balsam, cosmos, cockscomb, gaillardias, globe amaranth, marigolds,.morning glories, periwinkles, petunias, portulacas, salvia, strawflowers, and zinnias.

April Garden Chores

Planting. Where water can be supplied, all types of shrubs and trees can be set in permanent locations this month. April is a good time to begin landscaping.

Vegetables. Only experienced gardeners can hope to raise good crops of pole beans, peppers, eggplants, or sweet corn this late in the year. These are not listed on the planting calendar for April and are not recommended even for average gardeners, much less beginners.

Insects. Insects will start building up this month, with the rapid rising of the average temperature. Grasshoppers, especially, will be on the move. Watch out for aphids and leafhoppers among the vegetables and annuals that you have not yet harvested.

Diseases. You can expect fungus diseases to be bothersome from now on through summer. Dust rose bushes every two weeks with a rose dust. Give your mango trees another application of neutral copper spray if you want clean fruit in June. Spray fig trees with neutral copper once a month from now on through summer to keep down fig rust.

MAY

First Month of the Rainy Season

Although May is considered the first month of South Florida's rainy season, in some years it is as dry as March and April. On the average, we are entitled to about 6.03 inches of rain in May. In some years we get more, and in others we get much less. May of 1925 was the wettest May on record, with 18.66 inches of rain. The driest May was in 1941, when only .32 of an inch was recorded.

A number of tropical flowering trees are in full bloom this month, including *Cassia nodosa, Cassia fistula* (the golden shower tree), *Peltophorum inerme* (yellow poinciana), *Lagerstroemia speciosa* (queen's crape myrtle), and *Tabebuia pallida.* Crimson Lake bougainvillea may again burst out in full bloom this month, after blooming periodically since January.

May is a good month to plant trees and shrubbery. Wait to plant until after the first rainy spell wets the ground throroughly. Even then, be prepared to water the new plants because you may not see another drop of rain for two or three weeks. May is like that.

Many Floridians do heavy pruning after the first of May. When fertilized, and irrigated if necessary, plants come back this month; you may train them during succeeding months to form dense, bushy plants.

The treatment a plant gets after heavy pruning determines the type of shrub or tree it will develop into. New growth can be expected to be vigorous and "sky-seeking." If neglected, the pruned plants will soon be leggy and as ill-formed as they were before you pruned them. After you prune a plant, your work has just begun.

Take a croton plant, for instance. A few days after pruning, new buds will begin to swell near the tops of the cut-back stems and within two weeks new growth will begin to burst forth in abundance. Keep your plants well fed and well watered during this period of rapid, succulent growth. As each new twig gets about eight inches long, carefully pinch or cut out the top growing bud, just as you would for an annual plant with a tendency to bloom too early. Removal of this terminal bud will slow down the growth, that is true. But it will also promote branching. New growth will appear on the new twig below the point where the terminal bud was removed—not just one new bud, but usually several. And when the new twigs get as long as eight inches or so, remove the terminal bud from each of them. By the end of summer you will have dense, broadtopped crotons instead of tall, skinny plants with only two or three main stems. You can give this kind of treatment to many of your other plants, especially hibiscus.

Know Why You Prune

Pruning is necessary, but it is sometimes overdone and sometimes not done often enough. Before pruning a shrub, vine, or tree, always ask yourself why. Be sure you know the answer.

There seems to be an almost universal belief that pruning a plant will produce magic results, making a plant burst forth in rapid growth, bloom lavishly, or produce fruits in abundance. There's nothing like a good pruning, many believe, to make a sick plant get well. Extension Service agents, nurserymen, and garden editors often get questions like these: "My plants aren't growing well at all. Should I prune them?" "My mango tree didn't bloom last year. Should I prune it?" "The leaves on my hibiscus hedge are turning yellow and dropping. Would pruning stop this?"

Instead of helping tropical plants, unwise pruning can injure or even kill them. In the North it is customary to prune peaches and apples to induce production of fruit of uniform size for marketing. Other trees are pruned to promote vigor. Northern plants store up starches in their branches and roots. When you reduce the top, especially the smaller branches, you reduce the area that must be supplied with the stored food when the warmth of spring causes the buds to open. Such pruning, when done at the right time, results in vigorous new growth.

Tropical plants do not store up starches to the extent that northern plants do. Tropical plants use their food reserves in a continuing, year-round growth. Therefore, when you drastically reduce the top of a tropical tree, you set back the tree by reducing its capacity to produce food. Many people actually kill hibiscus by repeated heavy pruning.

Pruning should be done for one or more of the following purposes:

1. To control or influence the form of a plant.

2. To remove diseased, weak, or dead branches.

3. To develop a densely branched plant, where form or flower production is the aim.

4. To reduce the size of a tree for hurricane protection.

5. To balance the top with the root system when a tree or shrub is transplanted.

Often shrubs have to be pruned too frequently because

they are set in places too small for them or because they are set under windows or in front of porches or breezeways. Very often the problem should be solved by transplanting rather than by periodic pruning. Another homemade pruning problem occurs where trees or palms are planted beneath power or telephone lines. The city of Miami now requires that trees be planted behind the sidewalk rather than in the parkway between the sidewalk and the street.

When major pruning is necessary, do it in the spring. Moderate pruning is possible throughout the summer: when practical, you should finish your pruning by the middle of September. Avoid heavy fall or winter pruning. Growth is slow in South Florida during cool, dry weather, and severely pruned plants have difficulty making a comeback.

Always prune with sharp tools. When you remove large branches, exercise care so that splitting branches will not tear huge strips out of the bark of the main trunk of the tree. Here is the way to cut back a heavy branch.

First, saw off the branch about six inches from the main trunk, making the first cut on the underside of the branch until the weight of the branch begins to bind the saw. Then remove the saw and saw through from the top. Now saw off the short stub, remaining as close to the trunk as possible. Paint over the wound with a water-base pruning paint. Pruning paint is available at garden stores. Do not use paint that contains turpentine or thinning oils, as injury to the growing tissue surrounding the wound is likely to result.

"Hurricane preventive" pruning is one of our most important types of pruning. Huge or tall trees with heavy, burdensome limbs and awkward forms can be dangerous in strong winds. Keeping rapidly growing trees within bounds may save you grief when the wind gets up to seventy-five miles an hour and above. Ficus trees, especially, should be cut back periodically to keep them from getting dangerously large.

The local power company has been doing preventive pruning for several years, and it has paid off. Branches are kept out of power lines, and tall, willowy trees are cut back to lessen the danger of toppling. Awkward and diseased branches are cut out of trees near power lines. By careful, planned pruning you can keep your trees from becoming giants. You can do this kind of pruning periodically all year; and if you keep after your trees, especially the ficus, severe pruning is seldom necessary.

Tips on Pruning Special Plants

Here are a few tips on pruning a number of fruit trees and flowering tropical plants in South Florida:

Citrus. Remove dead or weak twigs at any time of the year. Also remove water sprouts (strong growth from the base of the trees or from branches) at any time of year. Otherwise, citrus requires little pruning. Remove awkward branches in February or March. If severe pruning is necessary, do it in May after the fruit has set. You will still have a crop of fruit on the remaining branches.

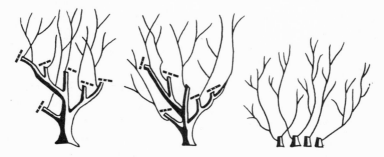

To improve the shape of a plant with a too tight or too open center, cut it back to where a branch or twig grows in the direction you want the plant to take. This side bud should point in this direction. To prune old shrubs (right), cut the main stem back near the ground where the branches begin emerging.

Avocados. Train avocados into bushy, low-growing trees rather than encourage tall and slender growth. An avocado is naturally rangy in appearance, and no matter how much pruning you do, it will never lend itself to formal shaping. Some varieties of avocados spread out naturally from the beginning, while others such as the Lula and Taylor grow naturally into slender trees. Prune avocados soon after they have set fruit, if drastic cutting back is necessary. Light pruning is all right any time of the year.

Mangos. Careful pruning is advised for these trees while they are young. When buying a young mango tree from a nursery select one with three or four well-formed, scaffolding branches. Refuse nursery trees that have been permitted to develop into two main branches forming a "Y." The "Y"-shaped tree, whether mango, avocado, or ornamental, is a hazard in the storm season, from June until fall. When heavy pruning is necessary, prune large trees between March and June or soon after the crop is harvested.

Poinsettias. Cut back leading branches after the flowers fade in late February or in March. Fertilize and water to induce new growth. Remove terminal buds from new growth after the growth has reached six or eight inches in length. This will induce additional branching. The idea is to develop a bushy plant by the time the flower buds begin to develop in late October. Prune your poinsettias for the last time in early September.

Hibiscus. There is entirely too much pruning of hibiscus. Train young plants to develop into bushy rather than tall and scraggly shrubs by removing terminal buds in young growth, as recommended for poinsettias. If excessively heavy pruning is necessary, do it after the first burst of spring flowering is over. Avoid pruning hibiscus in fall or winter.

Bougainvilleas. Do heavy pruning, when necessary, after bloom has finished in spring. The main reason for pruning bougainvilleas is to keep plants compact or to keep vines under control. These plants will bloom whether or not you prune them. You may periodically cut back long, heavy sprouts through the summer growing season so that by fall your main plant will have numerous large and small branches. Do no pruning after September. Feed heavily during the growing season but let up on feeding after September. Bougainvilleas flower best when on the "hungry and thirsty" side.

Propagate By Air Layering

Air layering is the easiest and most satisfactory method of propagation for most ornamental plants and for many fruit trees. Moreover, by air layering it is possible to produce fairly large plants, or even small trees, within a year. You can air layer, or "moss off," as large a branch of a tree as you can handle.

Air layering induces a branch of a plant to form roots in sphagnum or peat moss while it is still attached to the mother tree. After the roots develop, the "air layer" is

Air layered plants have a headstart on cuttings. To propagate by this method, remove a two-inch ring of bark from a year-old branch. Place damp sphagnum moss around the cut and cover with tightly fastened plastic. After roots develop, trim off branch, pot the new plant, and place it in shade for several weeks.

removed and planted first in a container to get it well established, then transferred to a permanent location in the garden. Most ornamental plants and a number of fruit trees can be air layered with ease, including hibiscus, guavas, bougainvilleas, rubber trees, most house plants, West Indian cherries, tamarinds, poincianas, and sea grapes, to name a few. Mangos and avocados air layer with difficulty, although in India nearly all mango propagation is done by air layering. But it takes experience in handling the newly air layered mango plants before the gardener can expect much success for the roots are extremely brittle.

As a starter, select a branch a little larger in diameter than a lead pencil. A foot or so from the tip, girdle the stem by ringing and removing the bark from an inch long area. Scrape the wood of the girdled area to keep the bark from growing back. Now take a handful of moist spagnum moss, wrap it around the girdled part of the stem, and cover it with a sheet of aluminum foil. Twist each end of the aluminum foil tightly around the stem in order to secure it well to the branch. You can buy sphagnum moss from garden supply stores and aluminum foil from grocery stores. You can use peat moss in the place of sphagnum, but it is more difficult to handle.

Tests have shown that you can cause roots to grow on some obstinate trees by applying root-inducing hormone to the girdled part of a stem. As in most other kinds of propagation, air layering works best during warm weather, from late spring to early fall. If you air layer during the cool season, select branches on the south side of the plant so that the "air layers" will be kept warm during the day. Heat induces rooting.

The sphagnum moss should be kept moist. At best roots develop very slowly when the sphagnum is permitted to dry out. When the moss is pretty well filled with roots, cut off the stem below the moss, remove the aluminum foil but not the moss, and set the new plant in a container of rich soil. Feed with soluble fertilizer and keep in a shaded location for a few days until the new plant gets used to being on its own. It is ready to be set in a permanent location after new roots have filled the container.

It's Also Time To Root Cuttings

May is also a good time to propagate ground cover plants in quantity, getting them ready to be set out in beds by the first of June. Wax-covered pasteboard milk cartons make excellent containers for starting such cuttings. Cut each container in half, making drainage holes in the bottom half. Four-inch clay pots also make good starter containers for ground covers. Many ground covers are popular in South Florida now and are becoming identified with the contemporary look. Best known is wedelia, a glossy leaved vine that bears a profusion of yellow, daisy-like flowers. It grows in almost any kind of soil, including marl; it will withstand salt spray and even a high salt content in the soil. New varieties of wedelia have been introduced and are being tried.

A tropical portulaca that thrives like a weed and produces flowers most of the year is also becoming popular. This plant, believed to be native to South America, was introduced here from Puerto Rico. There are several varieties bearing a number of different colors including yellow, pink, rust, and white. The plant looks much like the common annual portulaca but makes a more dense, vigorous plant, covering the ground to a depth of six or eight inches. It takes shearing well.

Several types of tradescantia are planted in South Florida from time to time, occasionally being "rediscovered" with a great deal of enthusiasm. It is a rapid grower and vigorous, doing very well in part shade or in full sun.

Nearly all of the ground covers are fairly easy to

propagate. You can set cuttings of most of them directly into beds, but for a few weeks while the plants are getting established and making growth, the beds appear new and incomplete. By propagating the plants first in containers and then transplanting to beds, you can make a show in a hurry. If you use milk containers, you can set the containers in the soil without disturbing the plants.

One ground cover that is not quite so easy to propagate is the shrubby cuphea. It can be grown from cuttings, but the expert will have much more success than the beginner. Take cuttings from vigorous plants in the spring or summer. Root in a mixture of coarse sand and one-fourth peat moss. Cuphea, because of its constant production of light violet flowers, makes an excellent ground cover in locations where there is no foot traffic. It really should be classed as a low shrub rather than a ground cover, and it can be used as such. Some landscape architects use cuphea in front of taller shrubs as a "facer" plant.

Many other ground covers can be used in special situations, such as the periwinkle for vacant, unused areas. Peperomia does well in shady locations where there is no foot traffic, and the same is true of a wide variety of ferns. Another group of plants deserving of attention are the common bryophyllums or kalanchoes, which grow in poor, sunny locations with little attention. They can be propagated easily from leaf cuttings. Ground covers seem to be getting increasingly popular, and nurserymen are constantly on the lookout for new varieties.

Soil preparation has a lot to do with the success of ground covers, expecially in new gardens where the soil is poor and lacking in humus. It is possible to prepare suitable planting beds by scattering a couple of inches of peat moss over the surface and "digging" it into the top six inches. About ten days before you're ready to plant, scatter six pounds of a garden type of fertilizer for each 100 square feet and wet it down with a sprinkler. You can hasten the growth of ground covers by weekly applications of a soluble fertilizer, applied with a garden hose attachment or with the aid of a sprinkler can.

Sand or Muck for Lawn Topdressing

By the first of May, grasses are beginning to come out of the lethargy induced by months of cool nights and dry weather. Homeowners, with new interest in their gardens, wonder whether to fertilize or put on a topsoil. If they decide to put on a topsoil, they wonder what kind to use.

Topdressings for lawns are overused in South Florida. Soil or sand should be applied to lawns for two purposes, to level rough areas and to take up the slack beneath spongy mats of grass. Fertilizer and water will take care of the growth problem. Where topdressing is needed, sand is usually the best choice. Muck is not recommended. Being organic and a poor quality organic material at that, muck oxidizes very rapidly and soon entirely disappears from the lawn. (Muck, however, is more satisfactory if it is mixed well with the soil prior to planting a new lawn.) Sand, being a mineral, is not lost when used as a topdressing; its use builds up the ground level permanently. Marl, which is mostly calcium carbonate or lime, is not recommended at all as a lawn top dressing. The ideal topdressing would be a sandy loam, pulverized and sterilized so that it's free of weed seed. But this is difficult to locate in Florida and unnecessary for good results.

Apply only enough of a topdressing to satisfy the needs of your lawn. The common practice of covering the lawn with a couple of inches of sand or other soil is very bad. The lawn grass is set back for weeks. Use just enough to take up the "slack" in the spongy grass. Scrub it into the soil with the back of a rake as you apply it.

If you apply a topdressing in May, it may be a good idea to wait until the first of June to fertilize. Even the whitest sand contains some plant food, enough to cause the grass to perk up. You may as well let your grass coast along a few weeks on this bit of plant food before you apply plant food that you have to buy in a garden store.

Use Insecticides Sparingly

With warm weather coming rapidly, insect pests will be on the increase during May. Chinch bugs will be multiplying and so will scale insects, caterpillars, grasshoppers, katydids, and a host of other bugs.

Not all the insects that visit the garden are harmful. In fact, the percentage of harmful insects among the tens of thousands of all insect species in the world is rather small. Most of the insects are harmless; some even come under the heading of "beneficial insects." This includes wasps and bees that most plants depend on for pollination and also the many predatory insects that live on other insects. Most of the insects you see buzzing around the flowers of mangos, citrus, or many ornamental plants do no harm. They are seeking nectar from the flowers. Unknowingly they carry pollen from blossom to blossom, accidentally fertilizing the flowers as they go. For this reason you should not apply insecticides to plants while they are in bloom or at least while insects are working among the flowers.

Reckless use of insecticides, without rhyme or reason, ordinarily kills more beneficial insects—pollinators and predators—than harmful ones. For this reason, do not apply the powerful insecticides except to control pests you know to be present. Except for the use of sulphur to control plant mites, it is not usually helpful to apply insecticides as a preventive measure. Sulphur has little effect on most beneficial insects.

Best known of the predatory insects is the ladybug. Both

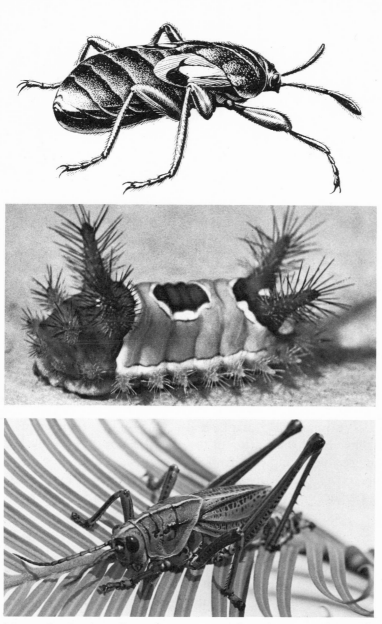

When selecting ingredients for pest control, seek expert advice. The procedure for eradicating the chinch bug (top) will not get rid of the poisonous saddleback caterpillar (middle) or the common lubber grasshopper (bottom).

the larvae and the adults feed on scale insects. There are lesser known insects that lay their eggs in the bodies of other insects, a practice known to insect specialists as "parasitism." Without enemies, some of the insects might become so numerous that they would threaten to take over the earth.

Japanese beetle, length: 1/2 inch

We often see such threats become near realities when an insect is accidentally introduced into a new country. An example is the Japanese beetle—an insect not considered a serious pest in Japan, where many insect enemies prey upon it. But in the United States, where it has no enemies to plague it, the Japanese beetle has annoyed farmers and gardeners for several years. Fortunately, the climate of South Florida is too warm for this beetle. Insect specialists are now fighting the Japanese beetle by bringing to this country its natural insect enemies from Japan. Since these insects do not feed on plants, there is no danger of their becoming pests.

Think about the relationship between the various kinds of insects when you go about spraying insecticides over your shrubs and fruit trees. Spray selectively. Watch out for pests on individual plants, and when you find them go after them. But do not attempt to spray the world. Not only is it impossible to get rid of every bug, it is not desirable. There are many useful insects that can be destroyed by reckless spraying.

May Weather Calendar

Following are the average temperature, rainfall, and wind velocity figures for a normal May in the Miami area.

Temperature. Average daily high: 85.4; average daily low: 70. Highest temperature ever recorded in Miami in May: 94 in 1956; lowest temperature: 50 in 1921.

Rainfall. Average: 6.03 inches. Wettest May: 18.66 inches in 1925. Driest May: .32 of an inch in 1941.

Wind. Prevailing direction from the east-southeast. Average velocity: 9.3 miles an hour. The highest wind ever recorded in Miami during May was 48 miles an hour in 1950.

Hurricanes. There have been no hurricanes in the Miami area during May.

May Planting Calendar

Vegetables. Collards, cowpeas, mustard, papayas, okra, peanuts, pumpkins, New Zealand spinach, squash, sweet potatoes, and turnips (for tops).

Annuals. Balsam, cosmos, cockscomb, four-o'clocks, globe amaranth, hollyhocks, marigolds, morning glories, periwinkles, petunias, salvia, and zinnias.

May Garden Chores

Propagation. Begin making new plants by air layering.

Pruning. Do major pruning this month. Cut back bougainvilleas, jasmines, crotons, and winter and spring bloomers that have passed the flowering stage. Fertilize after any heavy pruning.

Insects. Caterpillars are getting more plentiful, and scale insects are on the increase this month. A variety of insecticides, headed by Sevin, will kill caterpillars, but you will have to use malathion or oil emulsion to keep scale insects under control.

Lawns. Uneven or spongy lawns need a top dressing this month. Sand is preferred to muck, marl, or other types of weed-loaded soils. Also keep a close lookout for chinch bugs in Saint Augustine grass. They begin increasing in great numbers during May, especially if the weather is excessively warm and dry. Get the chinch bugs under control before they take over the lawn.

Planting. You can plant or transplant shrubs or trees this month, but be prepared to do a lot of watering if it doesn't rain.

JUNE

First Month of Summer

June is the first month of summer. The almanac tells us summer begins on June 21, the longest day in the year, and lasts until September 23. For all practical purposes, it is under way in South Florida by the time the first of June rolls around, and it remains with us somewhat past September twenty-third.

May is a pleasant month in Miami. May days are not uncomfortably hot, and May nights are pleasantly cool. Florida's tropic summer is in full swing from the beginning of June until about October 15, but it isn't the ordeal that newcomers may imagine. Actually the South Florida temperature never gets as high as the temperatures during short periods in northern cities. The daily high temperature for June is around 88 degrees, the daily average low temperature is 74 degrees. The highest temperature ever recorded in June was 95 in 1952. Even during our hottest spells, the nights are more pleasant than are the hot and sultry nights characteristic of heat waves in Washington and New York.

The high humidity doesn't have to be a problem in South Florida. Air conditioning is universal, and if you want to keep the windows open, fans will keep the air circulating for comfort. Outdoors, the almost constant trade winds from the Caribbean make patio and Florida room lounging enjoyable.

Time to Plant Fruit Trees

Most commercial growers in South Florida plant groves in June. Trees set out this month have five months to get established before the dry, cool season sets in after October. Homeowners will be wise to adopt this practice of commercial growers. Then during the dry season it will not be necessary to water established trees so often.

Ordinarily, you can expect to get about six and a half inches of rain during June. But, because you can never be certain, be prepared to water unless rains fall regularly. A newly set-out plant should get a soaking every few days for the first several weeks.

Nurserymen used to tell gardeners that it was better to plant a fifty cent tree in a five dollar hole than a five dollar tree in a fifty cent hole. Old-timers spent a great deal of time and energy in planting preparations. First, they would dig a hole many times bigger than the ball of tree roots. Into this hole they put several bushels of animal compost, plus rock phosphate and perhaps some well-seasoned chicken manure. All this they mixed with the topsoil removed from the hole. They planted the tree in the middle, watered it well, and then mulched it.

There's nothing wrong with this kind of tree planting preparation. The only catch is that good compost is hard to come by. Furthermore, labor is high when you buy it, and if you do it yourself it's rough on muscles. Fortunately such strenuous preparation is not necessary any more. You will find it helpful to mix a few pounds of superphosphate in the bottom of a planting hole. And you can add a quart of sheep manure to the soil you toss in about your young tree at the time of planting. But it is possible to grow good trees with the help of commercial fertilizer alone.

Just set your tree in the soil you have at the same depth that it grew in the nursery or in the container from which it was removed. Make a basin in the soil and let the young tree sit in the middle of it. The depression should be large enough to hold several gallons of water. Now water your tree until the soil is well soaked. Cover the soil with several inches of mulch. Water daily for a week, filling the hole with water each time. More newly planted trees are lost for lack of watering than for any other reason. Water newly planted shrubs or trees whether it rains or not unless at least an inch of rain falls. The home gardener is often misled by daily light rains. The top of the soil may be moist, but beneath the surface the soil may be bone dry. In the meantime, your newly planted tree may be suffering severe damage from a lack of moisture. Just be sure you don't let the soil become dry.

Nurserymen and grove owners fertilize young trees once a month in order to push them to rapid growth. A heaping handful of fertilizer may not be too much for a young tree three feet high that has been transplanted from a three-gallon can, the most common type of container nurserymen use for growing large plants. Scatter the fertilizer over the mulch and somewhat beyond. Never pile fertilizer near the trunk of a tree. When young trees—especially fruit trees—are pushed with monthly fertilizer applications it is a good idea to spray them periodically with nutritional spray. Apply the nutritional spray to your young growing trees every three months.

What Fruit Trees To Plant

There is a wide variety of fruit trees for planting in South Florida. It is possible to have fruit coming in at all seasons.

Mangos may be harvested from June until October, while avocados may be picked from dooryard trees from the middle of July until the following January and February. Limes mature in the summer and in the fall. Oranges mature from October until the middle of January, and some varieties will hang on the tree until as late as the end of March. The grapefruit, tangelo, tangerine, and Temple orange are winter-maturing fruits.

The colorful Haden has been Florida's most popular mango variety for nearly half a century. One of the earliest to come into production, its fruit matures in June and July. In recent years, however, other mangos have been developed that have become very popular. Today the mango grower can choose from more than a dozen very good varieties. The Irwin and the Zill come in a little after the Haden. The fruit of the Kent matures in July and August, and the fruit of the Keitt in August, September, and October. In selecting mango varieties for dooryard planting, don't be misled when making a choice for fruit quality. One of the least colorful of Mangos, the Carrie, is popular for dooryard planting. The Carrie is of no value as a commercial fruit since it must be left on the tree until it is mature or it does not develop a good flavor. Newcomers gaining in popularity include the Tommy Atkins, more disease-resistant, and Sabbath Jubilee. The Van Dyke, Ruby Red, Fascell, and Peach are also preferred by many.

There are dozens of varieties of avocados, planted both commercially and in dooryards. On the other hand, many very good dooryard avocados in South Florida are seedlings, grown from the seeds of fruit that people liked especially well. You can find a great many varieties of avocados in plant nurseries, but you will not go far wrong if you plant the following: Pollock, for July maturing; Waldin, for September; Booth 7, December; Linda, January; Choquette, February.

While considering possible fruit trees for dooryard planting, we should not overlook the lychee. A well-grown lychee
in full fruit is one of the most striking of all of our
ornamental plants, as well as our fruit trees. Even when not
in fruit, the evergreen lychee can be a handsome tree. Its
clusters of bright red fruit mature in May and June. The
Brewster variety, introduced from China, has been the most
popular variety for both commercial and dooryard planting
for more than half a century. A more recent introduction is
the Bengal, a lychee from India.

The lychee tree prefers a soil that is neutral or slightly
acid in reaction. With careful treatment the tree will grow
well in Dade County's limestone soil. The tree must be given
regular applications of a neutral iron in order to keep the
leaves green. The iron can be applied as a spray, or it may be
dusted on the leaves. Apply iron every time you apply
fertilizer. Also add iron to the foliage if new leaves do not
quickly develop a characteristically green color.

All nursery-produced lychees are propagated by air
layering. Once planted, a lychee tree cannot be neglected.
Even a mature tree should receive periodic irrigation during
dry weather. Bulletins and circulars on growing tropical
fruits may be obtained free of charge from your county
agent's office or from the Florida Cooperative Extension
Service, University of Florida, Gainesville, Florida, 32601.

No Dollars on Dooryard Trees

Dooryard fruit trees should be planted for the pleasure of
growing the trees and producing the fruit. You can forget
any idea you may have about planting a few mangos or a
few lychees to "pay the taxes." Those half-acre and
acre-sized fruit groves just don't pay off. In order to
produce fruit of commercial value, it is necessary to spray
regularly, to say nothing of applying fertilizer at the right

time. To produce marketable avocados or mangos, you would need to put on at least five applications of spray and perhaps more. You would have to apply insecticide sprays, fungicide sprays, and nutritional sprays. You would have to control scale insects, whitefly, and mites and keep fungus diseases off the fruits.

Federal marketing agreements limit the quality of certain fruits than can be shipped. At present the agreement applies to avocados and limes. Eventually it is likely to apply to the mango, if commercial growers get together and vote approval of a marketing agreement. Under rules set up through marketing agreements, shipping scabby or otherwise diseased fruits is forbidden. These marketing agreements apply to owners of half-acre as well as hundred-acre groves.

It may be possible for a homeowner to produce marketable fruits from a small grove, provided that he is willing to carry out a full program recommended by the county agriculture agent. To save money, he must be willing to do all of his own work. Even then, he can expect to get very small pay for his labor.

What Is the Best Lawn Grass?

When supplied with a minimum amount of fertilizer and kept free of insects, lawn grasses grow rapidly during the long and warm days of June. This is a good month to start new lawns or to change over from a grass with which you are dissatisfied to another variety. But reconsider before you change from the variety you are now growing, and reconsider three or four times before you plant the high-maintenance grasses many people are planting these days. By high-maintenance grasses I mean Bermuda and the various zoysia varieties.

I would be the last person to recommend any variety of

grass as the "best grass." Over the long pull, Saint Augustine has been about as satisfactory as any other grass for general planting. Many who shifted from Saint·Augustine to centipede during the early 1950s, when chinch bugs were destroying so many of Saint Augustine lawns, have since given up their centipede lawns and gone back to Saint Augustine. Of the various grasses planted in Florida, all of them are far from perfect. A grass that is suitable for a certain location may be an extremely poor grass under other circumstances. Take centipede grass, for instance. It is one of those "low maintenance" grasses that cannot stand prosperity. Centipede does fairly well if fertilized very lightly—it at all—and watered when it is thirsty. Ordinarily, centipede should not get more than fifteen pounds of a regular lawn fertilizer per thousand square feet of lawn space. Once a year is usually often enough to fertilize centipede. Apply the fertilizer in late October. If a second application is necessary, apply it in March or April. Do not fertilize centipede during the summer. After the fall application of fertilizer, spray the centipede lawn with either iron sulphate or neutral iron. Iron sulphate can be applied at the rate of one tablespoonful of iron sulphate to one gallon of water. When applied at this rate it will not burn the grass.

Recommendations for Fertilizers

Recommendations for high-maintenance lawns are just the opposite from those for centipede. Both Bermuda and zoysia must be fertilized several times a year if you are to keep them in top-top condition. When you fertilize these lawns, you may as well follow up immediately with an application of an insecticide for control of the armyworms or sod webworms that usually follow fertilizer applications made to any grass in the summertime.

Most homeowners fertilize Saint Augustine grass three times a year: in the fall immediately after the rainy season ends, then in January or February, and finally around May or June. The May or June application can probably be avoided and it is a good idea to avoid fertilizing Saint Augustine during the warm months. With two applications of fertilizer a year, Saint Augustine should look reasonably good all year. Much depends on the owner's attention to irrigation, to mowing, and to insect control.

Mowing is very important in maintaining a lawn. It is a common practice to wait until the grass badly needs mowing before cranking up the mower. The grass may then be cut so low that it is given a shock and a setback. During the summer growing season, it is a good idea to mow all lawns once a week, and Bermuda perhaps twice a week. Never remove all of the blades from the stems. Grass produces most of its food in its green leaves. To remove all of the leaves is to weaken the grass severely. For centipede and Saint Augustine the mower should be set so that the grass is cut about two inches high; the mower may be set somewhat lower for other grasses, depending on the frequency of mowing.

Most lawn grasses sprigged in June will cover the ground completely by the end of summer. The exception may be zoysia, a slow growing grass. Even zoysia may be made to cover completely if it is planted as closely as five inches apart and fertilized often. The secret in getting fast coverage is to fertilize every two weeks. Don't put down a heavy application each time. Make the first application of a complete lawn-type fertilizer. Apply at the rate of about thirty pounds per thousand square feet. Two weeks later apply ammonium sulphate at the rate of five pounds per thousand square feet. Any other type of nitrogen, such as forty percent neutral nitrogen, can be substituted. Follow the manufacturer's directions. Four weeks after the first application, repeat the complete garden fertilizer at the rate of twenty pounds per thousand square feet. Keep switching, complete fertilizer one time, nitrogen fertilizer the next, until your grass has covered the area desired. You'll have to do a lot of watering and a lot of spraying and dusting for insect control. The insects will be waiting to hop on your grass every time you fertilize, and you will have to be sharp to stay ahead of them.

When it is necessary to water, do it in the morning. Do not water in the late afternoon and evening. Irrigating late in the day sets up your grass for a fungus invasion because the fungus-attracting moisture evaporates more slowly at night. Once a fungus disease gets started in grass, it is very hard to stop. You may have to drench the lawn with a fungicide such as zineb every five days to get the fungus under control. Even that may not save your lawn.

The worst general pest on lawns during the summer is the sod webworm, which attacks all grasses. It is almost certain to follow summer applications of fertilizer. The sod webworm's favorite grasses seem to be zoysia and Bermuda, but this pest won't pass up lush Saint Augustine or centipede either. Scatterings of brown or dead spots that seem to appear in the lawn overnight are good signs of the presence of sod webworms. Armyworms work from the top, mowing off the tops of the grass while the sod webworms work from the bottom. A bad infestation of sod webworms can do severe injury to zoysia or Bermuda grass unless the pest is quickly brought under control. Sevin may be used to get rid of both sod webworms and armyworms.

Check Orchids This Month

Transfer orchids that need potting to fresh osmunda fern roots early in the summer, especially if you leave your plants out under slats where they must take the constant

In protected areas, orchids thrive out-of-doors throughout the year

pelting from rains during wet periods. You can give somewhat less attention to orchids potted in charcoal or some of the barks that have recently become popular. Unless orchids have perfect drainage, their roots may decay. Once decay starts, it may not stop until the entire plant has been killed.

The novice orchid grower will save money in the long run if he deals with an orchid grower who has had long experience. Despite the constantly advertised claims that orchids are easy to grow, there are many tricks in growing them. Orchid growing can be a very expensive hobby for the person who starts out in the dark and stays in the dark. Even the most experienced grower will have trouble with plants. Unless you know how to recognize trouble, such as damage from red spider or scale insects on leaves, or know the elementary do's and don'ts about watering, you may eventually find yourself in a peck of orchid troubles. There are several very good books on orchid growing. Along with your first orchid plant, you should buy one of these books and study it thoroughly. Knowing the theory of growing orchids is not enough, however. You must grow them yourself, and you must learn many of the tricks from experienced growers.

Colorful Fruits Ripening

Two of our most flavorsome and most colorful fruits begin to ripen this month: the mango, from India, and the lychee from China. The flavor of the lychee is hardly matched by that of any other fruit. Yet, strangely, because of its unusual flavor, many people have to learn to like the lychee. The flesh has the consistency, the juiciness, and the sweetness of a grape, but here the similarity between the two fruits ends. The best that can be said is that the lychee has a wonderful flavor of its own, one that defies description.

South Florida lychees are shipped to specialty stores across the U.S.

The flavor of the mango is better known. Yet few are familiar with the wide variation in flavor among the different varieties of mangos. Flavors and preferences vary. Each mango gourmet has his own choice varieties. You have to sample varieties until you find the one you like best.

Also ripening in June are the Ceylon peach, a tropical variety, and the West Indian cherry. Although the Ceylon peach was introduced into Florida more than sixty years ago, somebody is always "discovering" that peaches can be grown here despite claims to the contrary. Actually the Ceylon peach is very easy to grow and is usually grown from seed. The first peach in the United States to ripen in the spring, the Ceylon is a freestone peach with a very good flavor. The West Indian cherry bears several crops of fruit a year. The Subtropical Experiment Station at Homestead has selected a sweet variety that produced fruit nearly an inch in diameter. Actually the West Indian cherry is not a true cherry but a malpighia.

Hurricane Watch Begins

Although the hurricane season officially begins in June, no hurricane has ever hit Florida in June during this century. In fact, the highest winds ever recorded in Miami in June were under fifty miles an hour. Hurricanes do occasionally form in the Caribbean area during June, but they are usually small and seldom reach the mainland.

June Weather Calendar

Following are the average temperature, rainfall, and wind velocity figures for a normal June in Miami.

Temperature. Average daily high: 88.1; average daily low: 73.5. Highest temperature ever recorded in June: 95 in 1952; lowest temperature: 65, recorded both in 1920 and in 1950.

Rainfall. Average: 9.15 inches. Wettest June: 25.34 inches in 1930. Driest June: .07 of an inch in 1931.

Wind. Prevailing direction from the southeast. Average velocity: 8.2 miles an hour. Highest wind ever recorded during June in Miami: 48 miles an hour in 1936.

Hurricanes. No hurricane wind (75 miles an hour) has ever been recorded in Miami in June. June, however, is the first month of the official hurricane season.

June Planting Guide

Vegetables. Collards, cowpeas, okra, peanuts, New Zealand spinach, squash, and sweet potatoes.

Annuals. Cosmos, cockscomb, dianthus, gaillardias, salvia, strawflowers, and zinnias.

June Garden Chores

Lawns. This is a good month to plant grass. Get as much planted as possible this month so that you can have good coverage before the summer is over. Keep a sharp eye out for the yellow spots in Saint Augustine lawns, a sign of chinch bugs, and get these pests under control immediately after you find them. Call in a lawn pest exterminator or spray with Diazinon, VC-13, or Trithion, following directions carefully. Also watch out for sod webworms, pests common in all lawns, especially lawns that have been fertilized recently. These pests are easily controlled by Sevin.

Pruning. Shrubbery pruned earlier will begin to put out lots of new growth this month. Begin to pinch back tips of new growth to develop bushier plants. Robust poinsettia plants may have to be reduced considerably this month.

Propagation. Try to wind up all of your air layering this month. It is possible to air layer six-foot branches of rubber trees.

Fertilizing. Fertilize fruit trees and shrubbery this month. You may also have to fertilize Bermuda and zoysia grasses. Try to avoid fertilizing Saint Augustine unless the grass especially needs it. Do not fertilize centipede in the summer.

Diseases. Warm, rainy weather is a good time for fungus diseases to get started. Watch out for mildew in plant beds. Dusting with sulphur will aid in controlling this disease.

Orchids. Repot all orchids whose leads have reached the sides of their pots or whose old potting medium has rotted.

Insects. Watch out for a buildup of scale insects on your trees, especially citrus. Control with malathion and oil emulsion. Also distribute metaldehyde pellets in plant beds and greenhouses this month for the control of slugs.

JULY

Look for Comfort

To know South Florida you should live here through a hot, moist summer and a cool, sunny winter. Only then can you appreciate the vast differences in the area's climate. Summer lasts from June to October. It's the length of the hot weather that disturbs many new residents. Although temperatures may go higher in the North than in Miami, the northern heat waves last a few days or, at the most, only a few weeks. In Miami, however, the daytime temperature of 85 or above, along with high humidity, remains with us for months on end, dragging on through July, August, September, and part of October. During this period there is seldom a letup in the heat, which almost never permits the thermometer to drop below 70. Before the development of air conditioning, South Florida residents sweltered through the long hot months. Homes were not so well insulated as they are today, and unless a house was designed for the passage of the breeze, the indoors could be very uncomfortable. It was cooler outdoors, in the shade of trees or in an open patio in the evening, but often the mosquitoes were so numerous in summer that residents preferred to stay indoors, cooling off in front of an electric fan.

Thanks to air conditioning, the way of living in Florida has changed. Most homes, stores, banks, and offices are air conditioned. Even the malls of many shopping centers are cooled. Cars are air conditioned. If you don't mind being shut up, it is possible to spend the summer in air conditioned comfort, braving the heat only to move from house to car and from car to office or restaurant. For this reason many find living through the summer in Miami more comfortable than in the North where air conditioning is far from universal. Spending all your time in air-conditioned surroundings however, makes one a prisoner of a desire for comfort and to most people this is an unsatisfactory way of life.

There was a time, a few years ago, when architects designed homes that could be thrown wide open to permit the passage of summer breezes. The demand today is for compact houses that are less expensive to build and to air condition. Frequently a house built in South Florida today has a swimming pool with a connecting patio under screening.

The modern Florida home, therefore, demands a new approach to landscape design—to the selection and placement of trees and shrubbery. Trees should be arranged for visual comfort as well as for physical comfort. Roofs are likely to be sufficiently well insulated to cut out most of the summer heat that once penetrated the old, noninsulated roofs and caused many homes to be unpleasantly hot. Walls and patios, however, still need the shade of trees. Properly placed shade can reduce air conditioning costs. Other values of trees are more important for the individual. Trees, even on a small city lot, help to fill the need to be close to nature.

You can place trees properly only after you have studied the summer shade patterns. Shade, of course, starts on the west side of your house in the morning. It moves to the north during midday, and moves to the east in the afternoon. As the pattern of shade movement will show, you don't need to plant trees on the north side if you are merely seeking to shade the walls of your home. The most important sites for planting trees are southwest and west of the building. It is the afternoon sun that is most severe in South Florida. Place your trees so that by mid-afternoon they will cast their shadows on the west wall and over part of the roof. Unshaded west walls collect and store heat, holding it for several hours after the sun goes down. During the warmest time of the year, a South Florida home without air conditioning may not cool off until after midnight. Sitting in the middle of lots planted with shade trees still too small to help, they collect the heat of the sun and hold it.

Trees have more effect on the weather than you may realize. The leaves of trees absorb very little heat. They feel cool to the touch. A breeze passing through the shade of a tree or through the foliage of a tree is cool. Our prevailing breezes are from the southeast. It's a good idea to place a tree or two somewhere in the southeastern part of your lot where the breeze will pass through the foliage or through the shadow of the trees before it reaches your house.

Results of research done by the University of California prove the importance of shade. Observers found that the temperature of the bare ground surface, ranging from 136 to 152 degrees, dropped an average of 36 degrees in five minutes after the passage of the "shadow line."

Select the Tree You Like

The several species of ficus, or rubber trees, are the trees most widely planted for shade in South Florida. Remember that these trees have an aggressive root system; do not plant them close to septic tank drains or close to walks. It is difficult to grow grass under a ficus since the tree makes a very dense shade. When planted close to a house, a ficus can overwhelm the building within a few years. A program of annual pruning, however, will keep a ficus under control and also prevent it from becoming hurricane bait.

A much better tree for shade is the pongam, which grows rapidly and produces a dense shade. The pongam sheds its leaves once a year but quickly puts on new foliage. Probably the least messy of all shade trees is one that is seldom seen in cultivation—the native wild tamarind from the Florida Keys, *Lysiloma bahamensis*. Its leaves, though somewhat like the leaves of the royal poinciana, are smaller and shed less freely. The wild tamarind is a well-formed, compact tree. It is very easy to propagate by air layering. Nurserymen offer a wide variety of shade trees, large and small. Palms also make good shade when planted in groups. The coconut palm is among the most rapid growing of palms. From the standpoint of economy, the right coconut to plant is one that is old enough to have mature leaves but not old enough to have developed any wood in its trunk. While the coconut doesn't make a dense shade, the shade is sufficient to be effective. The palm is particularly good for an area that has a wet summer climate like that of South Florida. Palms let light through their fronds and permit air circulation, which helps prevent the mold-breeding conditions that are likely to develop in densely shaded areas during rainy weather. Grass also grows well beneath palms.

When selecting trees or palms for shade buy the largest you can. Even in South Florida, where plants grow most of the year, it may take many years for small plants to reach sufficient size to provide the shade you need.

Plan Garden for Living

It used to be customary to beautify the front of a home

and neglect the back. The backyard was sparsely edged with trees and shrubbery while the front yard became a show place, planted and cared for with the idea of making a pretty picture.

In the best landscape design of today the garden in the rear may get more attention than the front yard. Although the front is not neglected, it does not get the exclusive and pampered attention that it used to receive. The idea of a picture garden is something of the past. The front is treated primarily as an entrance with a driveway for the automobile or perhaps a court for several automobiles to park, a service entrance, and a main entrance for the owners and their guests. Modern landscaping calls for an uncluttered front, with more attention paid to developing an outdoors living area. Since most of us want privacy, the outdoor living area is usually located in the rear. The living area, beginning with a screened porch, Florida room, or a combination of both, opens into a patio of stone, gravel, or concrete. A shade tree or groups of palms furnish shade for the patio. Plastic-covered furniture offers year-round hospitality.

From the border of the patio spreads a green lawn, or perhaps shrubbery masses or ground covers, depending on the size of the garden and the special treatment the area demands. The patio and garden are enclosed by screening hedges or fences. The hedges can be formal and sheared, or they can be larger shrubs planted to provide a screening effect. At the proper places there are plantings of palms, large or small, perhaps a row of trees along a west boundary to provide afternoon shade, groups of crotons for leaf color, ground cover plantings of begonias, wedelia, or tradescantia as facer plants set before taller character plants or hedges. Combinations can be endless, just as the imagination of the individual has no limit.

Whether the planting arrangement is pleasing and the design good, bad, "cute," stiff, or offbeat depends on the talent, the experience, and the intelligence of the person who does the designing. No piece of ground is too small or too large for a garden. You just treat them differently. If you have a home on a farm, then the adjacent fields can be considered part of the landscape; so can a cattle pasture with cows grazing at a distance. The characteristic barn or silo may be an interesting part of the landscape. On the other hand, proper planting can convert the tiny city garden into a unique, livable spot. It's hard to imagine a backyard so small that it won't support a small shade tree, a hedge, border plants of rich shrubs, and lush, tropical ornamentals. There are plants for every purpose. The main problem lies in designing a garden in which these plants are used effectively from the standpoint of horticulture and landscape design. Landscape art, like any other art, is not easy. It is mastered only after several years of study. The homeowner, then, cannot expect to do a masterful job of landscape design unless he has knowledge of art and of horticulture. Many a homeowner has no knowledge of either. He buys plants from this nurseryman or that nurseryman and sets them out haphazardly.

You Can Do Your Own Landscaping

It's a good idea to have landscape plans drawn up immediately after your house plans are drawn. Patios and walks laid out in the landscape design can be poured by the building contractor. You then can go ahead with the rest of the landscaping in easy stages. If you know a little about gardening, you can do much of the planting yourself. In good design you must keep in mind ease of upkeep. This means an uncluttered lawn and grouping of shrubs and trees along the borders of the property. You must be extremely careful in determining trees and shrubs to plant about terraces or in the open lawn area. They must serve a definite purpose. The homeowner first must decide just what he wants. If he wants a large terrace or patio for outdoor living, the problem of providing privacy makes immediate demands. Large shrubs massed along the border of the property will insure privacy. Later, he can place low shrubs in front of these taller shrubs. Still later, he may perhaps plant various ground covers in beds marked by free flowing lines.

A landscape architect can also redesign a property incorporating many of the existing plants and trees. His fee will vary according to the size of the grounds and the amount of work involved, whether he takes full charge of the project, supervising the planting, or whether he provides the plans and leaves the work up to you. Many will also consider acting merely as a consultant without drawing up plans.

If you do not want to retain a landscape architect, you can still have a well-landscaped home provided you take the time to make a careful study of your lot and of the landscape materials that interest you. An amateur can become disheartened by the project if he tries to rush through his ideas without sufficient planning. You can pick up valuable pointers from county extension service booklets on landscaping and plant materials. Visiting botanical parks and attractions such as Fairchild Tropical Garden, Parrot Jungle, Sarasota Jungle Gardens, Cypress Gardens, Sunken Gardens in Saint Petersburg, and McKee's Jungle Gardens in Vero Beach will be helpful. A study of their patios, sunken gardens, the use of ground covers among palms and other trees, the placement of walks and driveways, and the use of open spaces should give you many ideas on how to organize your own landscape plans and which plants to use.

Ground Covers Becoming Popular

Recent trends in landscape design have brought about a demand for ground covers. Many new varieties, some of them spectacular in their effect, have been introduced and tested. The most outstanding ground cover introduction in recent years is *Setcresia tampiciana,* commonly known in the nursery trade as purple queen. It is very effective in large masses and has become a popular landscaping material.

The demand for ground covers, however, has caused nurserymen and landscape architects to reexamine some of the older plants suitable for such use. The idea of using large masses of plants has brought the common *Zebrina pendula,* known as wandering jew, back to popularity. Another oldtimer that has recently become popular is the purple oyster plant, *Rhoeo spathacea.*

Many plants heretofore grown only in the greenhouse are now being used as ground covers. One is the airplane plant, *Chlorophytum somosum.* Both green and varigated forms of this plant are being used. The common pothos is being used for ground cover where special effects are wanted. Such plants as the smaller-leaved philodendrons are used as

Zebrina is one of many highly decorative ground covers available.

ground covers to produce an atmosphere of tropical lushness.

The wedelia, which is as popular as ever, is especially good in the open sun. It does not produce flowers too well in the shade. Sprawling lantanas also make excellent ground covers. For deep-shaded locations ferns, liriope, and the common peperomia are excellent plants. For dry, hot locations there is no better plant than the several species of kalanchoes. They can be propagated from leaf cuttings. These plants should be replanted every year after they are through blooming.

Many of the ground covers, unfortunately, are subject to nematodes. If nematodes are suspected, treat the soil with one of the several nemacides on the market now. They really work. Nearly all the ground covers need well-drained soil. Drainage is more important than richness, although the soil should not be excessively poor. A coarse sand mixed with peat moss makes a good basis for growing ground covers. Feed the plants every two weeks with a soluble fertilizer. Most ground covers need constant attention. They are more susceptible to insect damage than other plants because they are low on the ground. They are especially subject to damage from slugs. A combination sulphur-zineb dust does a good job of keeping both insects and most diseases under control. The dust should be applied while the plants are dry, and every effort should be made to get the dust underneath the foliage, instead of merely depositing it on the upper surface of the leaves.

Keep That Lawn Well Mowed

Since lawn grasses grow rapidly during the long days of summer, mow regularly. If grass is neglected, it tends to grow straight up because of the competition to reach the light. Then, unless you set your mower rather high, you're likely to remove most of the grass blades. If you mow grass once a week, however, the blades tend to lie parallel to the ground, giving you a stronger grass and richer color.

It is a good idea to rake up grass clippings, especially when they pile up after mowing and tend to shade the grass. The accumulation of clippings is not good for a lawn because clippings tend to build up a mat of grass above the ground. Saint Augustine clippings not only provide a good place for chinch bugs to hide but also make a heavy mat through which it is hard to penetrate with insecticides. It is a simple matter to catch the clippings in a basket attached to the mower.

July Weather Calendar

Following are the average temperature, rainfall, and wind velocity figures for a normal July in Miami.

Temperature. Average daily high: 89.3; average daily low: 75. Highest temperature ever recorded for the month: 100 in 1942; lowest temperature: 65 in 1956.

Rainfall. Average: 7.19 inches. Wettest July: 15.33 inches in 1941. Driest July: .48 of an inch in 1932.

Wind. Prevailing direction from the southeast. Average velocity: 7.8 miles an hour. Highest wind ever recorded during the month in Miami: 53 miles an hour in 1936.

Hurricanes. There have not been any hurricanes in the Miami area in July, but there have been several near misses.

July Planting Calendar

Vegetables. Collards, cowpeas, okra, peanuts, New Zealand spinach, squash, and sweet potatoes.

Annuals. Cosmos, cockscomb, dianthus, gaillardias, salvia, strawflowers, verbenas, and zinnias.

July Garden Chores

Fertilizing. Continue to feed monthly any plants set out in May or June. Only by monthly feedings in South Florida's porous soil can plants be pushed along.

Houseplants. Fertilize houseplants at least twice a month if you want them to grow rapidly. Use a soluble plant food. There is danger of burning if you use a dry fertilizer.

Insects. There are likely to be more signs of chinch bug injury in Saint Augustine grass this month than in June. Apply insecticides as soon as you spot chinch bugs, and repeat in ten days to catch those that have hatched out in the meantime.

Propagation. Continue air layering and the rooting of cuttings this month if you need additional plants. This is also a good time to propagate new houseplants if your present ones are tall and leggy.

Fig trees. Begin spraying the foliage of fig trees with edible fruit with neutral copper to prevent fig rust, a disease that causes the leaves to drop. The more common inedible varieties have no problem with fig rust.

Fruit trees. If you did not give heavy-producing mangos and lychees a generous application of fertilizer in June, be sure to do so this month.

AUGUST

Time for Armchair Gardening

At the end of this chapter you'll find an August planting guide listing a number of vegetables and annual flowers that can be planted this month. After reading it, go take a dip in the swimming pool or relax with a tall glass of limeade. August is South Florida's hottest month. Yet the grass grows and the insect pests thrive. You'll find enough to do keeping the lawn mowed and the pests under control. So, if you are a newcomer, take a tip from the "Crackers." Take it easy. You'll need your energy to throw off the lethargy, to get outdoors and look for the pests—the chinch bugs and sod webworms in your grass, scale insects on fruit trees and ornamentals, aphids on the new growth of citrus, and the mites on your greenhouse plants.

It is possible to grow okra, squash, cantaloupe, turnip greens, collards, or a number of different kinds of annual flowers, but you would have to keep after the crops constantly with a combination of insecticides and fungicides to ward off insects and diseases. It isn't worth it. Wait until September to make seed beds, and be prepared to plant gardens in October.

Prior to 1964 South Floridians had reason to think the

area immune to August hurricanes. While it was no rarity for hurricanes to form during August somewhere in the Gulf of Mexico, Caribbean, or Atlantic, they veered away from Florida—until the night of August 27, 1964, when Cleo, after clouting Miami with winds of 120 miles an hour, moved up the east coast, leaving a wake of wreckage and proving you shouldn't be completely relaxed even if the statistics are overwhelmingly optimistic.

August is a good time to arm yourself with facts about gardening in South Florida. You can never know all there is to know about gardening—about the thousands of plants here, the actions of fertilizers, the nature of soils, or all the uncertainties about sprays. When you come face to face with problems that you haven't run into before, you can turn to many sources for information. Much of the information is free. Both the Florida Cooperative Extension Service at Gainesville and the Florida State Department of Agriculture at Tallahassee publish many free bulletins on gardening for Florida residents. Although no single book will answer all your gardening questions, there are a great many good books dealing with tropical plants and how to grow them. The largest display of such books in South Florida is probably at the Fairchild Tropical Garden. There you can see titles from India, tropical Africa, and Hawaii as well as from Florida. Members of the Fairchild Garden Association may borrow the books from the garden's lending library.

Despite all of the books on tropical gardening, many new and baffling problems arise from day to day to send the gardener to new sources in search of information. For instance, how does one go about getting a certain insect identified? Or to whom would you send a specimen of a strange flowering tree coming into bloom for the first time? The Division of Plant Industry, Florida Department of Agriculture, in Gainesville has an efficient, helpful staff of entomologists who can identify almost any insect you are likely to run across in Florida. Be sure to prepare the insect specimen so that it will reach its destination in good condition, not in a hundred pieces as sometimes happens when insects are mailed in an envelope. Send plant specimens—and specimens should include a twig complete with foliage and flowers or fruit intact—to the Herbarium, Agricultural Experiment Station, University of Florida, Gainesville. It is best to send tropical fruit specimens to the Subtropical Experiment Station, Homestead. The Dade County Extension Service office will answer general questions on gardening, such as the time for fertilizing grass or fruit trees, and can help you out with specific questions, too.

Garden supply stores can be very helpful. When you go into a garden store to buy an insecticide to kill bugs found on one of your citrus trees, take a twig covered with the insects along with you. Or if you want to get rid of a weed in your lawn, take a specimen along. Before leaving the store, be sure to get full directions on the use of insecticides or weed killers. If you need soil, fertilizer, or such services as spraying, it's a good idea to trade with firms or with individuals that have a permanent address where you can go and complain loud and long if you feel you have not received a fair deal. Do not buy from door-to-door salesmen offering bargains on sod, soil, or plants. The inferior quality of their products will cost you money in maintenance, and with their portable "offices," you'll have no chance to complain.

Visit Parks and Botanical Gardens

There's nothing like a botanical garden to help a newcomer to Florida get acquainted with the plants that are new to him. Dade County is especially rich in such gardens.

But there are many private gardens throughout South Florida, including the Caribbean Gardens at Naples, Cypress Gardens at Winter Haven, the gardens of the old Thomas A. Edison home at Ft. Myers, and the Jungle Gardens at Vero Beach, as well as the private collections that nurserymen develop. Often the nurseries are better sources of information about individual plants than are some of the large private gardens; the spectacular private gardens give you a chance to see how the plants are used to best advantage. Following is a list of gardens in Dade County that have worthwhile plant collections:

Fairchild Tropical Garden, 10901 Old Cutler Road, Coral Gables. Admission to nonmembers is $1; children under twelve with adults are admitted free. One of the outstanding tropical botanical gardens in the Western Hemisphere with a famous collection of palms, flowering trees, and vines. Open daily.

Fairchild Tropical Garden is a mecca for gardening enthusiasts throughout the tropics.

Watson Island's famous Japanese Garden draws gardeners looking for landscaping ideas.

Miami Beach Conservatory, 2000 Garden Center Drive, behind Miami Beach Convention Hall. Admission is free. Features collections of ferns, orchids, bromeliads, and shrubs.

Redland Fruit and Spice Park, 248th Street and Coconut Palm Drive, about five miles west of U.S. 1, Princeton. Free admission. A county-sponsored collection of 200 tropical and subtropical fruit trees from around the world.

Parrot Jungle, 11000 Southwest Fifty-seventh Avenue, Miami. Admission is charged. Outstanding collection of bromeliads. Many ideas for pool plantings and rock gardens.

Japanese Garden, Watson Island, Miami. Admission is

free. An oriental setting created from plants adapted to South Florida. Ideas for pool landscaping.

Orchid Jungle, 26715 Southwest 157 Avenue, Homestead. Admission is charged. A massive collection of orchids in a natural, twenty-five acre jungle hammock.

Matheson Hammock, on Old Cutler Road, Miami. A natural jungle of native Florida trees. The same plants are found in many tropical jungles in the West Indies, Mexico, and Central America. Open daily. No charge for admission.

Simpson Park, on South Miami Avenue at Seventeenth Road, Miami. A natural jungle of native Florida trees. Open daily. Free admission.

The Fairchild Tropical Garden has the most complete collection of tropical plants in Florida. Its collections of palms, cycads, and vines, all labeled, are among the best in the world. Every year the garden introduces many new tropical plants from all over the tropical world. Except for a few kept for planting in the garden itself, they are distributed among the members of the Fairchild Tropical Garden Association, whose contributions help keep the garden going. Memberships, which start at fifteen dollars a year, include a bulletin containing much information on tropical plants.

You'll Like the Palms

As a group, the palms are without doubt the most important and most popular ornamental plants in South Florida. There is hardly a garden in the area that does not have a few palms. The newcomer first gets acquainted with the coconut and the royal varieties and then perhaps with some of the smaller palms such as the adonidia and the Alexander. Unless he gets particularly interested in palms, he may never become acquainted with more than half a dozen species. However, more than three hundred species brought here from all over the world are now growing in South Florida.

Not all of the palms introduced have made the grade. Our climate is not tropical enough for the betel nut palm. Our elevation is not high enough for the Colombian wax palm of the Andes, and our rainfall is not sufficient all year for the stilt palms of the wet tropical jungles. Many other palms have failed to survive in Florida, possibly on account of the soil. We have never been able to establish the Cuban belly palm, *Colpothrinax wrightii,* in Florida. Small plants have been able to take rather low temperature, but they failed to survive for other reasons. It is possible that many palms failed to survive in Florida because of our limestone soil. They may prefer an acid soil. We know very little about the soil preferences of palms since science has never been called upon to make a special study of this problem.

Incidentally, Florida is the home of fewer than a dozen native palms. Florida's best known native palm is the sabal or cabbage palm, which grows in immense colonies in many parts of the state. This palm, which appears to be more subtropical than tropical, grows better in central Florida than in South Florida. It thrives along the east coast as far north as Virginia. Probably more plentiful than the sabal palm is the common palmetto, a palm with a reclining trunk that grows as a scrub in the pinewoods of Florida. This palm is so common that it is freely destroyed. As the palmetto becomes harder to find due to the widespread clearing of land, it is likely that many people will begin to save a few clumps when they clear their lots for building purposes. The palmetto looks very good when preserved in large clusters and surrounded by green grass. Scrub palmettos vary somewhat in color. Some have glaucous, gray-green fronds, whereas others have bright green fronds. The scrub palmetto is an extremely slow grower. It burns readily and makes a very hot fire because of the wax in the leaves, but it is the first plant to make a comeback in the pinewoods after fire has swept through.

One of the most widely planted palms for ornamental purposes is the thrinax palm of the Florida Keys. Many thousands of these tall and slender palms are being destroyed in the development of the Keys. They are especially easy to transplant if they are root-pruned a couple of months before being moved. If a rather large root system is taken with the palm, it may be moved successfully at any time without root pruning. But if most of the roots are destroyed in the transplanting, it is almost impossible to get this palm to live. Occasionally men have brought truckloads of these palms to the Miami area and sold them to gullible homeowners. The homeowners little suspected that the palms, chopped out of the soil with but a few roots, had no chance to survive.

Form Makes the Palm

In general, the beauty of the palm is in its form rather than in its color. It is true that a few palms have very colorful fruit, including the adonidia and the aiphanes, but the flowers themselves are never really colorful. The flowers are, however, spectacular because of their form and the number of individual flowers on a single inflorescence. The flower cluster of the tailpot, which blooms once and then dies, may weigh several hundred pounds. Palm flowers are usually cream or brown in color. Their decorative value lies in their form and interesting detail. Some hang like huge mops, such as the flowers of the fishtail palms and some may be as delicate as lace, as, for instance, the flowers of the *Trithrinax brasiliensis* of South America.

No other flowering plant is more striking in bloom than the sugar palm. The huge panicles hang eight feet, each streamer holding hundreds of flowers. Enormous numbers of bees and wasps buzz among them, making a continuous

Palms display their variety of form in three basic types: from top, the fan-shaped leaves of the cabbage palm, the gracefully drooping fishtail palm, and the feather-leaved Canary Island date palm.

*Paurotis palms grown in clusters illustrate the
effectiveness of grouping small trees.*

hum. Individual flowers drop as they mature and spend
themselves, accumulating on a conical mound below,
dropping, dropping, dropping, like continuous drips of rain.
The mound grows until, days later, it is more than two feet
high. The mound may contain two or even more bushels of
bloom.

The sugar palm, like the fishtail palm, begins to bloom only after it has reached maturity. The first bloom forms in a leaf axil near the top of the palm. Bloom clusters appear progressively lower, at each old leaf scar, until in time the lowest panicles touch the ground. After the final bloom appears, the palm dies. But the sugar palm may be fifteen or twenty years old before the first bloom begins, and it may live for two or three years while in the process of blooming.

The odor of palm flowers may be agreeable to some people and disagreeable to others. The fragrance of the cabbage palm flower is sweet and strong. Its slightly musty odor is too much for some people, but palm flowers are not known to cause hay fever.

The nectar of palm flowers makes excellent honey. Cabbage palm honey is widely popular although the flavor is somewhat strong for one who prefers a mild flavor like that of thistle or clover honey. Coconut honey, which is milder than cabbage palm honey, is sometimes offered on the Miami market.

Most palms are fairly easy to grow. Except for a few of the cluster palms, especially the raphis, palms are propagated from seed, never from cuttings. Leaves stuck into the ground will not form roots, as newcomers to Florida occasionally learn for themselves. In planting seeds, barely cover them with soil. Some sprout within a few weeks. Others may take much longer, while a few, such as the orbignya, may take two or three years to sprout. None of the commonly grown palm seeds take this long to sprout. When pushed along with plenty of water and fertilizer palms are rapid growers. They may seem to be very slow growing while tiny seedlings, but once they have formed considerable leaf surface they start growing in a hurry.

Many people, including some experienced landscape architects, have difficulty in using palms in the landscape. Except where a special effect is desirable, it is no longer considered good landscape practice to set palms in rows along the border of a sidewalk or driveway. Nor it it good practice to set them helter-skelter about the lawn. It would be difficult to advise anyone just how to go about placing palms in a garden. Every situation is different, and what may be good for one place may not be good for another. The small to medium-sized palms are more suitable for the small city lot than large palms, such as the royal or the huge West Indian sabals. Sometimes cluster palms can be used for screening, especially for large grounds. If small trees or large shrubs are used for hedging or screening, then it may be possible to plant groups of single-trunked palms effectively in front of these plants. As the palms grow up, they can be included in a bed of ground covers extending as far back as the border of the hedge. For instance, groups or single specimens of cocos plumosa, adonidia, Alexander palms, or hurricane palms (*Dictyosperma album*) can be planted along the border of the garden, not far out from hedges or other plants used for screening. Later, these palms can be taken into beds and enclosed within free flowing lines, making irregular scalloped patterns of ground covers or other rich foliage plants around the border of the garden. To carry out such a scheme would require very careful planting and perhaps the assistance of a landscape architect. If shade trees are used, palms should not be planted close to them because the two types of plants are bound to interfere with each other eventually.

Learn Preventive Pest Control

There's no better time than August to get used to the idea of using preventive measures for control of insects and diseases on ornamentals. Farmers accepted the "ounce of prevention" idea several years ago. Many gardeners are beginning to learn that the same idea works well for them.

Suppose you plan to plant a bed of roses this fall. The chances are that you will be advised to spray or dust once a week as a precautionary measure against insects and diseases. Perhaps you may wonder why. "Why not wait and see," you may ask yourself, "whether the plants show signs of insects or diseases? " You should not wait until you see those unwanted signs for the leaves of a rose bush can be severely damaged by mildew or leaf spot before you notice any trouble and the leaves can be seriously damaged by spider mites without the owner ever seeing one of these tiny pests. If the plants are dusted or sprayed every week or so with a combination insecticide-fungicide preparation, pests or diseases will have little chance to get started. The foliage will stay healthy and the plants will grow well and produce abundantly

The worst enemy of rose growers in Florida is black spot. Leaves turn progressively yellow and spotted unless regular spraying is followed.

Unfortunately, preventive control measures have not been developed for all pests. There are no methods for preventing chinch bug infestation. You will have to keep on your toes and catch these fellows as soon as they get started in your lawn; otherwise they will do extensive damage. Scientists are working hard to develop preventive control measures for a wide number of insects and diseases. They have already developed quite a number. For instance, farmers spray tomatoes every five days with a fungicide-insecticide combination for control of insects and the fungus disease called late blight. Citrus growers dust or spray regularly with sulphur or other miticides for the control of rust mites. Commercial orchid growers spray their plants with miticides such as Dimite or Aramite for the control of red spider mites.

The wide-awake gardener, especially one who follows gardening as a hobby, should keep up with the latest developments in the control of insects and diseases in ornamentals. The growing of disease-free and insect-free ornamentals adds immeasurably to the pleasure of Florida gardening.

August Weather Calendar

Following are the average temperature, rainfall, and wind velocity figures for a normal August in Miami.

Temperature. Average daily high: 90; average daily low: 75.3. Highest temperature ever recorded in August: 98 in 1954; lowest temperature: 66 in 1950.

Rainfall. Average: 7.03 inches. Wettest August: 16.88 inches in 1943. Driest August: 1.15 inches in 1938.

Wind. Prevailing direction from the southeast. Average velocity: 7.5 miles an hour. Highest wind ever recorded during the month in Miami: 74 miles an hour in 1964.

Hurricanes. August is a prime month for hurricanes. The most recent one was Cleo in 1964.

August Planting Guide

Vegetables. Carrots, cowpeas, cucumbers, celery, leaf lettuce, mustard, okra, peppers, squash, and turnips.

Annuals. Asters, balsam, cosmos, cockscomb, dianthus, forget-me-nots, gaillardias, marigolds, periwinkles, petunias, phlox, portulacas, salvia, scabiosa, tithonias, verbenas, and zinnias.

August Garden Chores

Propagation. Continue air layering this month. Make this the last month for dividing tropical bulb plants such as amaryllis or crinums.

Lawns. Unless you are pushing newly sprigged grass in order to get coverage of your lawn in a hurry, do not fertilize grass this month. If you do fertilize, be ready to follow up immediately with Sevin for the control of sod webworms or armyworms.

Insects. Get all insects cleaned up this month from fruit trees and ornamentals. Check especially for whitefly. Malathion and oil emulsion combined make a first class insecticidal mixture for the control of most of these insects. Use sulphur to check whitefly on papayas.

Diseases. Watch for fungus on leaves of soft-foliage plants and rust disease on leaves of fig trees. Neutral copper will control fig rust and most other diseases.

Pruning. Check weak and awkward branches on trees that may become hurricane bait during September and October when we're most likely to have a hard blow. It won't hurt to cut back heavy tree crowns this month. It's better than to have the high winds do it.

SEPTEMBER

A New Season Begins

Just as spring marks the beginning of the gardening season in the North, so fall marks the beginning of the gardening season in South Florida. September is the month when we make our gardening plans, thumb through seed catalogs, start our first seed flats, and turn the first spade of soil to make a garden.

"Continued warm and scattered showers" is a normal weather prediction for the first day of September. People fan themselves, cows seek the shade, and at midday bass may refuse to be drawn from cover by fancy lures, but the first swallows of the season have arrived from the North. These little fellows can't read a weather prediction, but like the first robin of spring in New England, they know as well as the weatherman that the swing of the seasons is underway. There are only twenty-two days left of summer. Cooler weather will soon be with us. By the end of October, the rainy season will be over too. Cool, dry weather will usher in South Florida's farming and gardening season.

September is the last full month of hot weather. Although the weather may feel sultry and uncomfortable throughout much of the month, and you may be ready to argue that it is just as hot as August, the temperature is from day to day getting cooler. The average daily high of September is somewhere around 88 degrees.

This Is Hurricane Season

September is the month of the big blows in Florida. On an average, homeowners will have to protect their property against hurricane winds of seventy-five miles an hour or more once in every ten years, according to weather bureau figures.

Any tropical storm within 2,000 miles of Florida seems to be a threat to this area until it has moved up the Atlantic or into the Gulf of Mexico away from the peninsula. We take the news of a new storm calmly enough. The hurricane forecasters give each storm a feminine name, such as Amy or Anna for the first storm of the season, Bernice or Bertha for the second, and so on down the alphabet. Half a dozen or more storms may be spotted and charted each season (June until the end of October). A great many of them never come near land. They originate far out in the Atlantic, and although they may take a course toward Florida for a day or two, they usually turn northward. We lose interest in a storm when it veers away from us. A week or so later we read in our newspaper about a "terrific storm" that battered ships in the North Atlantic, or swept over Nova Scotia, or even hit far-off Iceland.

Floridians follow the course of a new storm with eager interest as long as it is a threat to this area. Storm advisories are broadcast over radio and television every four hours. If a storm approaches the Florida coast, the weather bureau may issue hourly bulletins on its progress. You make a quick check to see that your storm shutters are in good shape and that a hammer and saw and other needed things, such as a step ladder, are where you can lay your hands on them instantly if you have to put up storm shutters in a hurry. Housewives check the food shelves and see that there is fuel for the kerosene lamps. If a storm should hit, power may be off for several days. Everybody keeps the radio on and waits eagerly for further advisories and bulletins. Eventually a new advisory is broadcast. And what does the advisory say? "The severe tropical storm, Emogene, is veering to the north and at the present time offers no threat to the Atlantic coast." Once again Floridians relax and return to normal activities. There have been times, though, when the storm didn't change course but kept on coming, like a missile from a gigantic weather gun aimed true at the Florida coast. They hit with terrific force, as history attests. And in the future other storms are likely to hit.

September Is One of Wettest Months

Besides being the month for dangerous hurricanes, September is one of South Florida's wettest months. In a normal September, you can expect nearly a foot of rain to fall. In some years there may be more, in others less. More than 24 inches of rain fell at Miami during September of 1960. Never since weather bureau records have been kept has less than two inches of rain fallen in Miami during September.

No matter how much rain may fall, you can step outside your house immediately following a shower and walk through your garden without having to wade through mud. Only where homes are built in low and unprotected areas subject to periodic flooding do you find muddy or soggy gardens. On the ridge of rocky limestone soil extending from Miami southwestward to Homestead, or in the sandy ridge that runs along the east coast north of Miami, you'll never encounter mud after a rain, a fact that makes South Florida one of the unique places in the world. The soil is very porous. Rainfall disappears beneath the surface almost as rapidly as it comes down.

In the Everglades and other low places, it is a different story after heavy rainfall. The glades become alive with animal life not apparent when sawgrass country is dry. Frogs suddenly appear in great numbers. They chirrup, peep, croak, or bellow, as befits the dignity of their size and species, while they abandon themselves to a noisy courtship. Soon the shallow water is teeming with millions of tadpoles. Meanwhile alligators, turtles, snakes, and fish desert the ponds and drainage canals to go exploring. After the frogs and fish go the egrets, herons, and wood ibis. Hawks circle overhead, their sharp eyes alert for a rabbit or rat clinging to a piece of flotsam or perched as helplessly in a clump of sawgrass. Little animals that the hawks miss, the owls are sure to get when they take over the hunt at nightfall. As the rain falls, farmers pump the water from their dike-protected farms while looking at the sky and wondering whether they'll be able to plant fall crops on time.

It is truly a subnormal year when anyone complains about a lack of rain during September. It is a good month to plant grass, transplant shrubs and trees, or get plants started that were air layered in late July or August. It's not uncommon for showers to fall on twenty of the thirty days in the month. Weeds grow abundantly. You complain about how fast the grass grows and how often you must mow it. Insects, such as armyworms and other caterpillars, plague the gardener.

Armyworm, length: 2 inches

Florida fern caterpillar, length: 1 and 1/2 inches

Push Young Trees with Fertilizer

Plants grow rapidly during the wet season, especially if the soil is good or if they are fertilized regularly. Young plants need monthly feeding if you wish to push them. When rainfall is heavy, young plants can be fertilized twice a month. If your soil is low and not well drained during rainy weather, better not plant such sensitive plants as avocados, hibiscus, papayas, and crotons. Plants vary a great deal in their tolerance of flooding or of soggy soil, as well as in their tolerance of excessive dryness or salt spray. The avocado is an example of an intolerant plant. It won't live in excessively wet soil, nor will it thrive near the ocean where flying salt spray may be blown onto its leaves. On the other extreme is the mangrove, which thrives in flooded salt marshes but refuses to grow on high land or in freshwater swamps. The coconut palm also will withstand salt spray and even tidal water lapping at its feet. Then there are trees like the bischofia, jambolan plum, and melaleuca, which will thrive for long periods in flooded soil. Even in families of trees there is a great variation among species in their tolerance to unfavorable conditions. Most rubber trees like fairly well-drained soil, but one member of this group, the giant fig from Malaya, *Ficus retusa,* will grow in wet locations or in brackish coastal marshes. You can never look at a plant and guess correctly whether it will live under varied soil and moisture conditions or in different climates. Take, for example, the Texas silverleaf, *Leucophyllum texanum,* which seems to do almost as well in Florida's humid climate as it does in the arid country of west Texas. One of Florida's most popular wetland trees, the tall and graceful melaleuca, is native to a dry part of Australia. Yet it now grows wild in the Everglades where water stands over its roots for months on end. The only way horticulturists can determine how adaptable a plant may be is to test it. Take advantage of their work by consulting a gardening book, nurseryman, or county extension service agent before undertaking experiments with unfamiliar plants.

Not Much Bloom but Plenty of Fruit

Trees and shrubs are in lush growth in September but bloom very little. Flowers that appear during the height of the rainy season, like the everblooming hibiscus or the ixora, may lack the rich color of flowers produced during dry weather. You'll see bloom in September, some here and there, such as the torchlike flowers of the dwarf poinciana or the weedy yellow elder with its drooping heads of golden flowers. You may see the night-blooming cereus break forth in its spectacular bloom, in one of its several blooming sprees during the year. Some of the species of lagerstroemia are covered with spikes of lavender flowers during September.

You may not think of September as a time when any important fruit is ripening, yet some varieties of both mangos and avocados ripen during the month. September is also the main season for guavas. Two important mangos, the latest of the year, ripen this month. They are the Brooks and the Keitt. The Brooks mango wouldn't rate a second glance during the season when the Haden and other popular Indian types of mangos are ripening, but any mango tastes good in September. The Keitt ripens in August to September. The Brooks is an old mango. The original tree grew from a seed planted by a Negro named Brooks in Miami about 1910. The Keitt, a newcomer, grew from a seed planted in 1939 on the property of Mrs. N. J. Keitt in Homestead.

Two good avocados mature in September, the Trapp and the Waldin. They follow the Pollock, which matures in July and August. The Trapp (no longer available in most nurseries) is older than Miami, and the Waldin (a superior variety) is nearly as old. A smooth-skinned fruit, oval in shape, the Trapp originated about 1894 on the property of H. A. Trapp in Coconut Grove. Its flesh is a rich yellow in color and of excellent flavor. Like the Trapp, the Waldin is smooth skinned, but it is oblong in shape with a characteristic flattening on one side of the blossom end. It originated on the property of B. A. Waldin, Homestead, from a seed planted in 1909. The flavor is excellent. The Trapp and the Waldin each weigh, on the average, about a pound.

Plant Vegetable and Annual Seeds

This is the month to plan the fall garden and plant vegetable and annual flower seed beds. The planting calendar is wide open, as you will find by checking the September planting guide at the end of this chapter.

Farmers like to make seed beds in newly cleared land free of soil diseases, nematodes, and insects. City dwellers can give young seedlings a good start by planting in seed flats or in other containers.

The soil used for planting seeds should be made free of diseases and insect pests by fumigation or some other kind of sterilization. If you intend to grow only a few plants in a clay pot, you can sterilize the soil in the oven. Put half an inch of water in the bottom of a large container. Then fill the container with soil and put it in the oven at 160 degrees F. Steam rising through the soil will sterilize it thoroughly.

Buy new clay pots for planting your seeds. Don't take a chance by using old containers that may be infested with insects, such as nematodes, and carry the spores of plant-killing fungi that cause damping off, a diseased condition of young seedlings.

If you do not have what you consider a good soil, you can prepare your own by mixing one part of peat moss in three parts of sand. But take no chance. Sterilize as already suggested.

Plant seeds in the soil according to directions on the seed packages. After the heads of young plants begin to push their way through the top of the soil, apply a soluble fertilizer twice a week. Make the fertilizer solution no stronger than the manufacturer's directions call for. Young plants should be grown in full sunshine. If set in shade, they will become spindly and weak, falling over when you plant them in your garden. Sun-grown plants are always better. Sure, they're more difficult to grow, but not much. Just keep them moist. You may have to water every day. But when you get ready to transplant your seedlings to permanent locations, all you have to do is dump them out of the pots and separate the plants. If you set them out with care and water them well, they'll start right off in full sunshine. And when you can grow plants like that, well, your friends will look on you as a real "green thumb" gardener.

Space, energy, and know-how are about the only limitations to the numbers and varieties of annual flowers you can grow in South Florida during the cool part of the year. Those new to gardening will do well to start with zinnias or marigolds, and perhaps calendulas. The work of plant breeders has made the zinnia one of the most outstanding of annual flowers. You can buy a hundred varieties of zinnias, from pigmy plants with quarter-size blooms to giant plants that produce flowers eight inches across.

Both zinnias and marigolds grow rapidly and come into bloom early if you treat them right, the first blooms appearing in about two months. Other two-month bloomers are alyssum, cosmos, and balsam. Coming into bloom in ten weeks are the periwinkle, Mexican sunflower, bachelor's button, black-eyed susan, and cockscomb. About two weeks later, baby's breath, calendula, dahlia, gaillardia, nasturtium, torenia, and stock begin to bloom.

While September is the time to get plants started, October is the time to plant them in permanent locations. We discuss soil preparation for gardens and plant beds in the October chapter.

Look out for Insect Pests

Plants that put out lush, tender growth during the warm, wet season become highly attractive to insects. Keep a sharp lookout for aphids on new leaves, armyworms and sod webworms on nitrogen-gorged leaves, leaf rollers on bougainvilleas, snails and slugs in plant beds and greenhouses, fat tomato hornworms on poinsettias, wooly caterpillars on your favorite shrubs, and scale insects and sooty mold on the leaves of avocado, mango, and citrus trees. It is fairly easy to kill these insects with Sevin, Diazinon, or malathion. Armyworms and sod webworms are discouraged particularly well with Sevin applied as soon as they appear.

Sevin will also take care of soft, armoured, and cotton-cushiony scale insects, as will a mixture of malathion and oil emulsion. The malathion-oil mix is effective on mites and white flies, too. Add to a gallon of water one teaspoonful of malathion and two teaspoonsful of oil emulsion. For soft plants such as African violets, you should not use the emulsion. Instead, use a malathion powder in water, to which a "spreader" has been added. The spreader acts like a soap or detergent, causing the material to spread out over leaves in a thin, even film.

It is a common practice to use heavier than recommended doses of insecticides on lawns in South Florida. While the lawn grass is tolerant to heavy insecticide mixtures, other plants may be burned badly unless you follow the manufacturers' directions. This is especially true for ornamentals.

Scale insects may escape the eyes of the inexperienced gardener, but these small, flat pests that attach themselves to leaves and stems can do much damage, injuring a plant by sucking the juices from it. They can cause a plant to shed its leaves and, in extreme cases, even cause the death of a plant where no control measures are practiced.

Even experienced gardeners are likely to overlook plant mites, commonly known as spider mites. These insects are so tiny that they can hardly be seen by the unaided eye. Under a magnifying glass they look much like spiders. The most common of plant mites is the red spider, more easily spotted than others because of its bright color.

Spider mite, length: 1/50 inch

Spider mites are sucking insects. They move about over plant surfaces to puncture leaves and stems and remove plant juices. After they have built up in rather large populations, it is easy to see the numerous small, discolored spots they make on leaves. Unfortunately, by that time they have already caused a great deal of injury.

Preventive measures are the best safeguard against spider mites. Spray house plants, especially orchids, once every couple of months with Aramite. Sulphur, an effective material that is cheaper than Aramite, will control rust mites and red spider on citrus and avocados.

Slugs, those large, slimy relatives of the snails, do more damage in gardens than most people realize. They frequently do the damage for which caterpillars and other insects are blamed. The slugs feed at night and leave only slimy trails as evidence of their visits. Bait containing metaldehyde will get rid of them and also millipedes. A metaldehyde bait with arsenate added in a concentration below three percent will get rid of snails.

Millipede, length: 1 inch

In preparing for war on insects, let's not overlook the chinch bug. This pest has cost South Florida homeowners several million dollars since the end of World War II. During some years the pest was so numerous that it was hard for homeowners to keep a lawn of Saint Augustine grass, the favorite food of this pest. Replanted lawns were immediately reinvaded. For many people drastic measures didn't work. Eventually it was recognized that the effectiveness of an insecticide on chinch bugs depended as much on how it was applied as how much was applied. Diazinon, VC-13, or Trithion are currently being recommended for the control of chinch bugs in this area.

Last Time to Prune Poinsettias

Give poinsettias their final cutting back in early September. Reduce the top from one-third to one-half. Cut each branch back some. Make the plant look more like a hatrack than a stub. Don't cut back any farther than you think is necessary. You'll have to be the judge of how far to cut back. If your plants are robust, with large trunks and strong branches, you needn't reduce the top as much as you should if the plants are weak and spindly.

After pruning give the plants a shot of fertilizer, and water it in. Any kind of general-purpose garden fertilizer seems to be all right for the September application. But be prepared to give the plants a high potash fertilizer at the end of October.

When new foliage begins to show after pruning, keep a sharp eye out for those big hornworms that like poinsettias so well. Half a dozen of these worms can denude your plants in a couple of days. Look for the eaten foliage and then for the worm. Spray with Sevin.

Poinsettias begin putting on flower buds after the middle of October. That's why it is necessary to do your final pruning at the beginning of September. Since the best flowers are produced at the tips of healthy branches, encourage your plants to make as many branches as possible.

September is also the final month for pruning bougainvilleas. These plants should not be drastically pruned after the early part of summer. The September pruning should be done only for the removal of awkward growth.

September Weather Calendar

Following are the average temperature, rainfall, and wind velocity figures for a normal September in the Miami area.

Temperature. Average daily high: 88.4; average daily low: 74.7. Highest temperature ever recorded in September: 95 in 1954; lowest temperature: 67 in 1938 and 1939.

Rainfall. Average: 8.96 inches. Wettest September: 24.40 inches in 1960. Driest September: 2.08 inches in 1912.

Wind. Prevailing direction from the east-southeast. Average velocity: 8.1 miles an hour. During the 1926 hurricane a wind speed of 126 miles an hour was recorded.

Hurricanes. Florida has its biggest storms this month. Chances of hurricane winds hitting your garden in September: probably once in ten years.

September Planting Guide

Herbs. Many of your favorite herbs can be grown in South Florida during the cool months. Seeds of anise, basil, borage, chervil, marjoram, sesame, and thyme can be planted now.

Vegetables. Beans, beets, broccoli, Brussels sprouts, cabbage, Chinese cabbage, carrots, cauliflower, collards, cucumbers, eggplants, escarole, kale, lettuce, mustard, onion sets, parsley, garden peas, peppers, radishes, romaine, rutabagas, spinach, squash, sweet corn, Swiss chard, tomatoes, and turnips.

Annuals. Asters, baby's breath, bachelor's buttons, balsam, calendulas, candytuft, carnations, cosmos, cockscomb, daisies, dianthus, forget-me-nots, gaillardias, globe aramanth, hollyhocks, lace flowers, lobelias, lupins, marigolds, nasturtiums, salvias, scabiosa, snapdragons, statice, stock, strawflowers, sweet peas, sweet william, verbenas, and zinnias.

September Garden Chores

Lawns. Armyworms and sod webworms may attack

South Florida lawns and pastures in tremendous numbers during September. They feed on the blades of grass. A number of insecticides are effective against caterpillars, but Sevin is the most widely used.

Poinsettias. They must be cut back early in the month. Poinsettias begin blooming in November. To wait until October to cut them back may delay the bloom. Cut back one-third to one-half, never back to a stub. Fertilize.

Bougainvillea. Do no drastic pruning of bougainvillea this late in the year. Trimming back some won't hurt, but do it early in the month. If you don't want unsightly vines by the time they are ready to put on bloom, keep a look out for caterpillars. They can chew up the leaves and make the plants look ragged and sometimes even bare of foliage.

Citrus. It's easier to get scale insects under control in September than later in the year. When they build up in large colonies, they remove so much of the plant juices from the leaves that the leaves drop. Malathion used with oil emulsion does a good job of killing scale insects. Use at the rate of one tablespoonful of fifty percent emulsifiable malathion and two tablespoonsful of oil emulsion to one gallon of water.

Roses. If you intend to plant roses this year, get the beds ready by the end of September. Use the richest soil you can buy. Some nurserymen sell rose soil. Better still, use a mushroom soil, available from South Florida mushroom growers.

Centipede grass. Keep mowed to prevent seeding. If centipede turns excessively yellow during the rainy season, don't be too hasty to apply fertilizer. Iron is probably needed, not nitrogen. Apply neutral iron or iron sulphate at the rate of one level teaspoonful per gallon of water.

Land crabs. These fellows are on the move in September, coming out of the water in great numbers and hunting for homes on the land. Kill them in their burrows with phosphorus bait applied to pieces of lettuce or cabbage. Stuff the poisoned leaves into the burrows. Both remedies are sold by garden supply stores.

Air layerings. If you intend to do any of this kind of propagating before cool weather arrives, better get your air layers on now. Air layered plants don't root very well in the cool, dry weather that we'll experience in the months ahead.

Papayas. Don't let these plants get hungry now while their fruits are sizing up. These are heavy feeding plants, requiring fertilizer every month for best results.

Bulbs. Plant any you can buy in garden stores. Amaryllis, callas, gladiolus, tuberoses, lilies, and zephyranthes can be planted now.

Fertilizing. Avoid fertilizing during this rainy month, except young plants that you want to push along by feeding monthly.

Pruning. Do final pruning this month, including especially the cutting back of poinsettias and final trimming of bougainvilleas.

Insects. This can be one of the worst months for pests. Watch out for a quick buildup of mealybugs, scale insects, and various kinds of caterpillars. Check mangos for presence of red-banded thrips, pests that leave their signs along the ribs on the undersides of leaves.

OCTOBER

End of the Rainy Season

If you haven't done so already, now is the time to get out the gardening tools and put a sharp edge on them. Despite the fact that the leaves on the trees remain green, fall is here and cool, dry weather is just around the corner. September may be the month when we plan our fall and winter garden in South Florida, but we do the planting in October. October marks the end of the rainy season and the end of the storm season. We usually get as much rain in October as we get in September, but most of the rain falls during the first half of the month. By the time November rolls around, we're normally at the beginning of our six-month dry season.

Farmers in many sections of South Florida have been in their fields for several weeks, plowing and planting. Soon the fall and winter vegetable season will be in full swing, with truck-loads of Florida-grown beans, tomatoes, peppers, and other winter crops moving northward.

Is It Really Soil?

Newcomers never cease to be amazed that anything can

be grown in some of the earth that natives and "natural-ized" Floridians affectionately call soil. Almost all of the Florida earth will produce crops if given the right kind of treatment. Even that gray sand of the flatwoods, the low cement-colored soil of the marl glades, or the rocky limestone soil of south Dade County can be coaxed with fertilizer to produce good crops for farmers. The same stuff in your backyard will turn out more tomatoes, beans, and cabbage than you and your family can eat. It will grow green grass, fine shrubs, or large trees. During the cool months, this Florida "soil" will grow almost all of the annuals that you grew successfully in the North. The secret of successful gardening in subtropical Florida is fertilizer—plenty of it—and water when needed. In the fall, when gardens are started, there is usually enough rainfall to get vegetables and annual plants underway. But after the end of October and from November right on to the following May, you will have to do a great deal of watering to grow fine plants in your garden. Never plant a garden on high land beyond the reach of the garden hose or some other kind of irrigating equipment.

If your garden plot is small, broadcast fertilizer over the entire area. Bulletins and books on gardening usually recommend broadcasting about three pounds of fertilizer for every one hundred square feet of garden space—a ten-by-ten area. But for the poor soil here, it is advisable to double, preferably to triple, this recommendation. Seven or eight pounds of fertilizer to one hundred square feet of space is not too much in South Florida's sandy or limestone soil. Apply the fertilizer after spading the soil and raking it clean of debris. Rake the fertilizer into the top two inches of the soil, and let a sprinkler play over the area for awhile to dissolve the fertilizer. The garden should be prepared and fertilized at least a week before you are ready to put in your plants or to sow seeds. This rule also applies to making flower or rose beds.

Where there is little humus in the soil, it may be advisable to add peat moss. Spread about two inches of peat moss over the soil and dig it under with a spade or fork. Be sure that the peat is thoroughly mixed with the soil. Peat aids in holding moisture and prevents some leaching of fertilizer during irrigation or heavy rainfall.

How to Garden on Rock

If you were to try growing vegetables or flowers in the rocky soil of south Dade County without preparing it first, you would have a difficult time, especially in areas where only one or two inches of sand lies over the almost solid rock. One easy way to overcome this problem is to build in a garden plot with narrow concrete blocks and fill the area with six or eight inches of soil. If the soil doesn't contain as much humus as you think it should, scatter an inch of peat moss over the surface and mix it well. A twelve-by-twenty-foot area will give you two hundred and forty square feet of growing space. With intense cultivation, you can grow all the vegetables and cut flowers that you can possibly use.

If your soil is full of weed seeds, you can eliminate them by applying a fumigant such as Vapam. Apply the Vapam about two weeks before you are ready to plant, being careful to follow the manufacturer's directions.

Now you are ready for planting. Some gardeners find it helpful to plan their gardens on paper before doing the planting, then lay off rows with a string running between two sticks. Obviously, not all vegetables or annuals grow best in rows spaced the same distance apart. You'll find recommended planting distances and cultural directions on every seed package you buy.

Order Strawberry Plants Early

October is the month for planting strawberries; the middle of the month is the best time. Set the plants in the ground as soon as you can after October fifteenth. To be sure to get plants at this date, order them in advance from your nurseryman or garden supply man.

If you plant the Florida 90 strawberry, you will need about a hundred plants in order to harvest between a pint and a quart of berries a day for several months. Prepare your strawberry patch as you would a vegetable garden or flower bed by distributing seven or eight pounds of fertilizer over each one hundred square feet of space. Scratch the fertilizer into the soil with the rake, then wet the plot down by running a sprinkler over it for awhile. You may want to fumigate your soil with Vapam to get rid of any weed seeds before planting. This must be done about two weeks in advance. Fertilize about ten days before time for your plants to arrive. Then set Florida 90 plants about fourteen inches apart and in rows at least two feet apart.

Strawberry plants are set too high if the roots show above the soil, too low if the bud is covered. Water well. Include a soluble fertilizer with the first irrigation water. Add the soluble fertilizer weekly until the end of three weeks, after which you can make an application of 6-6-6 garden fertilizer. Scatter the dry fertilizer on each side of the rows about eight inches from the plants. Fertilize thereafter at six-week intervals and scatter the fertilizer in the middle between the rows, for by this time the roots will have traveled that far.

Rose Planting Season Is Coming

While you are in the mood for working in the garden, October is a good month to get the rose beds ready if you intend to plant roses in November. If you buy roses grown in containers, it doesn't matter much whether you plant them in October or November. If you intend to buy plants dug from the fields of Texas, Tennessee, or New York, however, you must wait until dormant plants are available. Dormancy takes place after the first frost, as any former northern gardener knows.

There are several ways to make a rose bed. The best way is to buy special rose soil from a nurseryman. You can make up your own soil. You'll need enough peat moss to cover the area three inches deep, a bag of garden fertilizer, and several pounds of sheep manure. Scatter peat over the plot where you intend to plant roses. Add a half pound of sheep manure for each rose plant you intend to set out, and then scatter over the area two pounds of fertilizer to each ten square feet of area. Work all of this into the soil thoroughly and wet it down well. Fumigate with Vapam. Let it stand for about four weeks. Turn the soil again before setting out your rose bushes. If you don't have the energy, the time, or the ambition to spend this much time making rose beds, you can still have fine rose bushes. Nurserymen sell plants in five-gallon cans. The plants will give you roses throughout the winter and spring, and after they are through blooming you can toss them out.

Fertilize Your Lawn and Shrubs

Many people fertilize their grass, fruit trees, and shrubbery in October, and the end of the month is usually the best time. It is especially important to wait until the end of the rainy season to fertilize grass. Fertilizing a lawn in the middle of the rainy season is sure to result in a crop of armyworms. You can wait as late as November fifteenth to fertilize your lawn if you wish. Mature shrubs and trees can be fertilized at the same time you fertilize your grass, or you can fertilize larger plants in late October and grass during the first two weeks of November.

You may not want to fertilize your mature fruit trees at this time. If your avocado, citrus, lychee, or other fruit trees bore heavy crops this year, then be sure they get a good application of fertilizer this month. If the trees did not bear heavy crops this year and if they appear green and healthy, you can skip the October application. It is not advisable to give bearing-size mango trees a large application of fertilizer during the fall. If the trees look good, do not fertilize them at all at this time of the year. It is a common practice to make no fertilizer applications to bearing-size mango trees from the time of the early summer application until the first bloom panicles begin to appear. The mango usually begins to bloom in December or January. Fertilizer requirements vary widely according to plant types and their ages. Half a pound of fertilizer may be enough for a healthy head-high croton. But twenty-five pounds is not too much for a fifteen-year-old avocado tree about twenty feet tall. As for grass, the common practice is to apply twenty to thirty pounds of a regular lawn fertilizer to every thousand square feet. This recommendation is for Saint Augustine, Bermuda, or zoysia. Apply no more than fifteen pounds per thousand square feet to centipede or Bahia.

If you have bare areas in your lawn that need a temporary grass over winter, you can plant Italian rye seeds this month. Winter rye is widely planted in South Florida each year, mostly in October and November. It is easy to grow if you fertilize your soil first and keep the rye seeds irrigated until they are well established. If the soil is extremely poor, distribute twenty to thirty pounds of fertilizer per thousand square feet. Wet it down well and wait a couple of days before planting. Plant at the rate of one pound of rye per hundred square feet if you want a thick stand. Rake the rye seeds into the soil and irrigate. If the lawn is newly sprigged and grass runners prevent you from using a rake, then just scatter a little sand over the rye seeds. Keep the seeds moist or they will not sprout.

Once you plant rye, you are committed to a winter program that calls for regular irrigation and regular mowing. Rye is a vigorous grass in winter while your permanent grass will be semidormant. Consequently, if you don't watch out the rye may smother your permanent grass. The rye will last through the winter, dying when warm weather returns.

If you followed the practice of cutting your grass very low last summer, set the blade of your lawnmower somewhat higher now. The growth of grass begins to slow down as the shorter days and cooler nights of November approach, and if you mow the lawn very close, the grass will have difficulty in recovering. To scalp your lawn at this time of the year is to invite disaster.

Contrary to popular belief, both zoysia and centipede must be mowed quite often. During rapid growth, zoysia should be mowed at least once a week and centipede once every two weeks. These grasses will need to be mowed periodically throughout the winter if they are kept watered and in good growing condition.

Because grass recovers slowly when damaged during cool weather, it is important to have the cutting blades of your mower sharpened at this time of year, especially if you use a rotary mower. A dull blade can do severe damage to your grass. Rotary mowers are not recommended for zoysia lawns. If you do use a rotary mower on zoysia, be sure to keep the blade very sharp.

Don't Pamper Bougainvillea

If you are among those who can never make your bougainvillea bloom, maybe you pamper your plants too much. An overfed and overwatered bougainvillea probably won't put on much bloom. In Central America where bougainvilleas really put on a spectacular show, the plants receive no water or fertilizer during the dry season, which begins in November and lasts until May. Even though the plants get so dry that they shed their leaves, they produce astounding masses of bloom. The colorful vines sprawl over houses, fences, and even over other plants.

If you fertilized your bougainvillea vines last summer and they have put on a healthy growth, do not give them any water or nitrogen-rich fertilizer this fall. At the end of October you may give your bougainvillea a fertilizer that is very high in potash and very low in nitrogen. Garden supply stores can sell you the mixture you will need.

A small caterpillar that rolls up the edges of leaves may give your bougainvilleas trouble at this time of year. At the first signs of these pests, spray the vines with Sevin. Add a spreader to the spray, so that the liquid will stick to the leaves. The insecticide will give better effects if applied late in the day, as the pests are night feeders. The caterpillars must feed on the insecticide-covered leaves before the poisons can take effect. Therefore be sure to give the plants good coverage.

Insects and Insecticides

While on the subject of spraying, it may be a good idea to reemphasize the necessity for thorough coverage when you apply an insecticide. Insecticides have little effect unless applied correctly. Ever notice how water rolls up and runs off the waxy surface of leaves? Insecticides will too unless you use a chemical that causes your spray to spread out over the leaf surface in a thin film. This chemical is variously called a "spreader," a "sticker," or a "sticker-spreader." Add it to all spray materials except when you're using oil emulsion. When applying a spray be sure that both the upper and under surfaces of the leaves are covered with the material. The spray must be applied with some pressure.

October is Cooler

The difference may be only a few cooler nights, but October isn't as warm as September. In October we have the last of the sultry weather of summer. The average temperature for October is around 77 degrees compared with 82 degrees for September and 83 degrees for August. Toward the end of October a chill is possible. Often a cold spell drifting down the peninsula from the white North makes a fire feel good in the late October evenings.

We've had a few bad hurricanes in Florida during October. The worst tropical storm we ever had during the month didn't even bring winds of hurricane force (seventy-five miles an hour), but its rains almost destroyed us. The 1947 storm brought rains that gave South Florida one of its worst floods in history, dumping a fantastic amount of water on the southeast coast. Within a few hours from ten to fourteen inches of rain fell along the edge of the Everglades from Homestead to Palm Beach County. Miami Springs and much of Hialeah were under water. So was Davie in Broward County. Everglades water backed up into Fort Lauderdale. Many old groves in south Dade County were flooded, and avocado and lime trees were killed. Pastures were flooded. Farmers, cattlemen, and dairymen suffered severe losses.

The flood caused damage amounting to millions of dollars and led to Congressional approval of a 200 million dollar flood control program for southeast Florida. Plans for this immense project were begun in 1948 by the U.S. Army Corps of Engineers, and work was still in progress in 1970 after many revisions and an expenditure of over 300 million dollars. Its works were designed to prevent disastrous floods as well as to relieve the area from long winter and spring droughts. Works consist of thousands of miles of levees and canals, enormous pumps, spillways, and salt locks, as well as over 2,000 square miles of water conservation and storage areas in the upper Saint Johns River basin, Lake Okeechobee, and three conservation areas in the Everglades. When completed, the project will be one of the largest of its kind in the world. Operations of the complicated and interrelated project is the responsibility of a state agency, the Central and Southern Florida Flood Control District, whose headquarters is in West Palm Beach.

October Weather Calendar

Following are the average temperature, rainfall, and wind velocity figures for a normal January in the Miami area.

Temperature. Average daily high: 84.6; average daily low: 70.7. Highest temperature ever recorded for the month: 93 in 1939; lowest temperature: 51 in 1943.

Rainfall. Average: 8.41 inches. Wettest October: 25.02 inches in 1924. Driest October: 1.12 inches in 1925.

Wind. Prevailing direction from the east-northeast. Average velocity: 9.1 miles an hour. A wind of 122 miles an hour was recorded in the 1950 hurricane.

Hurricanes. Chances for a big blow are about the same in October as in September.

October Planting Calendar

Vegetables. Cabbage, celery, Chinese cabbage, carrots, collards, cucumbers, escarole, kale, leek, lettuce, mustard, okra, onions, parsley, parsnips, peppers, pumpkins, rhubarb, romaine, rutabagas, sage, spinach, squash, sweet corn, Swiss chard, tomatoes, and turnips.

Flowers. Asters, baby's breath, bachelor's buttons, balsam, calendulas, candytuft, carnations, cosmos, cockscomb, daisies, dianthus, forget-me-nots, gaillardias, globe ama- ranth, hollyhocks, lace flowers, lobelias, lupins, marigolds, nasturtiums, pansies, periwinkles, petunias, phlox, poppies, portulacas, salvias, scabiosa, snapdragons, statice, stock, strawflowers, sweet peas, sweet william, verbenas, and zinnias.

Bulbs. Amaryllis, callas, eucharis, gladiolus, gloriosas, lilies, narcissus, and zephyranthes.

October Garden Chores

Lawns. Keep watch for armyworms. Fertilize grass if needed, but wait until the end of the month. Spray centipede with neutral iron if you did not do so in September.

Poinsettias. Give these plants an application of fertilizer if their leaves are not a dark green.

Citrus. Check for scale insects and get them under control early in month.

Roses. Make beds for planting in November.

Strawberries. Plant as soon as possible after October 15.

Herbs. Most herbs can be planted this month. Try garden supply stores for seeds.

Pruning. Postpone heavy pruning until next spring.

Fertilizing. Plants that need it can be fertilized between October 15 and November 1.

Insects. This can be a bad month for caterpillars, armyworms, and cutworms. Control them with Sevin. Ants and cutworms may be routed with Sevin or Diazinon. Try Kepone on mole crickets.

*Mole
cricket,
length:
1 and 1/2 inches*

*Cutworm,
length:
1 and 1/2 inch*

NOVEMBER

Best Time of the Year

November ushers in one of the most pleasant parts of the year in South Florida. Normally, November brings cool, dry weather that stays with us for six months. November weather is nearly six degrees cooler than August weather. Before the month is over, South Florida can expect a visit from that unwanted unadvertised-for tourist from the North, Jack Frost. Frost often crosses the state line in October, and by the end of November may reach the outskirts of Miami. We have no record of frost in downtown Miami during November; but when frost forms in the Everglades, it's cold in Miami, often reaching the lower 40s. The weather warms up rapidly after the sun gets up, and by ten o'clock on a "frosty" morning, Miami Beach may be crowded with bathers.

Although you may now feel fall in the air in Miami, the place to "see" fall in November is in the Everglades and the pinewoods. The grasses have finished blooming and are now turning brown. The scrub willows in the glades have shed most of their leaves. Soon they will be as bare of foliage as though they were in Boston Common or Central Park. And so will the cypresses and red maples in Big Cypress Swamp along the Tamiami Trail.

First Month of Dry Season

Records show that an average of about two inches of rain is usual in November. But the month can be very wet. A total of 21.08 inches of rain fell during November 1952.

We have had one hurricane in November. It hit Miami on November 4, 1935, and was a good one, with gusts of wind up to 150 miles an hour. This unusual storm was bred somewhere out in the Atlantic beyond the Bahamas and headed up the Atlantic toward Cape Hatteras. But just before it got to Hatteras, the storm stopped. After resting awhile, it turned and made a beeline to Miami, not swerving a hair's breadth until its center arrived at the intersection of Miami Avenue and Flagler Street. It did damage totaling millions of dollars and gave Miami's trees their most thorough pruning since 1926.

You can go picnicking or fishing in November without having to worry too much about mosquitoes. Most mosquitoes have disappeared by the beginning of November, and we don't have to start slapping again until the following June. It's a good month to fish in Florida's lakes and streams and a good month to camp out. The nights are cool and a campfire feels good.

Feathered Tourists Head Southward

Florida's skies are busy in the fall with tens of thousands of migratory birds winging their way from summer nesting grounds to a warmer winter climate. Not men, but birds first discovered the Florida peninsula as a connecting link between the Americas. Millions of years before Will Rogers described Miami as the "jumping off place" of North America, birds were winging their way down the peninsula in the fall and "jumping off" for the West Indies and Central and South America. In the spring birds use Florida's airways again, on their way back north for a brief nesting period. Migration reaches its peak in November. During these periods of mass migration, many thousands of birds may be in the air at the same time, flying night and day. Observers have reported watching mass flights of ducks for several hours before the last duck passed overhead. Not all migratory birds fly nonstop over Florida. Just as planes may land in Miami briefly on their way farther south, many birds stop over on the peninsula. The same birds will stop over on their return flight north. A great many migratory birds stay in Florida through the winter, just as tourists do.

Some migratory birds don't like even mildly cold weather. A drop below fifty degrees will send them scurrying to warmer climes. Severe cold waves, which occasionally dip into Florida, have caught swallows before they could get away, leaving thousands of them dead from "freezing." Robins, on the other hand, don't seem to mind the frosty weather common in the southern states. Severely cold winters, however, drive robins to Miami by the thousands. Sometimes they come to South Florida in such numbers that they have difficulty getting enough food. During these periods they give strawberry growers a fit. "Robin winters" in Miami reflect much colder weather in the rest of the state.

Many of the birds that live in Florida or visit the state at different times of the year are not a bit backward about accepting handouts of food. Homeowners have learned that by providing feeding stations and water they can attract all kinds of small birds, keeping the garden alive with their activity, song, and color. The interest in feeding birds is well illustrated by the amount of wild bird seed sold in the Miami area during the fall and winter—more than three tons a week.

Birds, like people, have their likes and dislikes so far as food is concerned. Seeds that attract one bird may not attract others. Some birds like tiny seeds, while others will take only the larger seeds, such as sunflower seeds. In general, only seed-eating birds will visit feeding stations offering nothing but grain. This group of birds includes the cardinals, sparrows, bluejays, and other thick-beaked birds that are capable of cracking seeds. Insect-eating birds, such as woodpeckers, warblers, and mockingbirds, are more readily attracted by feed containing animal proteins. A few birds, like bluejays, will eat almost anything.

Feeding stations should be situated out of the reach of cats. Feeding birds on the ground is an invitation to neighborhood cats to hang around waiting for a free meal, too. Water should also be provided for birds.

If you have plenty of shrubbery and trees, you will have many birds whether you feed them or not. Warblers like live oaks and especially wild fig trees, both of which attract the tiny insects on which small birds feed.

Tomatoes for Christmas

Those who planted gardens early will have large plants coming along now. Tomatoes will soon be blooming if they are not already. The first radishes can now be harvested, for radishes are ready about three weeks after planting. Home-owners new at gardening often are surprised to see how big radishes will get when left in the ground—sometimes ten or fifteen pounds. A radish that big isn't tasty, however, and can't even qualify as an oddity since far heftier ones have been recorded. Don't wait to see how big a specimen you can grow of this or any other vegetable if taste is your main interest. Harvest them when they're young and in their prime.

Aphid,
length:
3/32 inch

Don't let the noticeably cooler weather of November lull you into the belief that garden insects will disappear. Maybe the mosquitoes have fled, but not the aphids or the beetles, cutworms, cabbage worms, corn earworms, leaf miners, mole crickets, leafhoppers, and leaf rollers. Keep a sharp eye out for a buildup of garden pests. They can come in a hurry. Sevin will keep them pretty well under control. Use no insecticides that contain oil on vegetables. Use a wettable powder to mix spray materials rather than an emulsion form of the insecticide. If you can't buy a wettable powder at your garden supply store, use a dust instead. If you will go over your plants once a week with a dust, you won't have much trouble from insects.

If you plant pole beans, as many persons do in South Florida, better dust once a week with sulphur to keep down rust. Once rust postules get started on the leaves of pole bean plants, they're hard to get under control. When grown well, the pole bean is one of the most satisfactory garden crops for South Florida.

Sweet corn is another excellent garden crop for South Florida, but in order to grow good corn you must have plenty of space and spend both time and energy on the plants. Few crops require so much attention. Garden varieties recommended by seed stores usually are more flavorsome than commercial varieties.

Plant sweet corn in November, December, and January. Fungus diseases are likely to attack corn planted earlier than November or later than January. A week before planting, distribute fertilizer over your corn plot at the rate of eight pounds per 100 square feet. If you want to fertilize at the time of planting, there is another procedure you can follow. Stretch a string along the row to be planted. Four inches on each side make a trench about two inches deep. Apply fertilizer in each trench at the rate of a one pound coffee can full for each fifteen feet of row. Cover with soil. Now make a trench beneath the string about one and one-half inches deep. Plant corn grains four inches apart in the row and cover. Moisten the soil with a light irrigation.

It takes plenty of fertilizer to grow good corn in Florida,

as it does for any other crop. Don't bother to get your soil tested. You can feel pretty certain that it will need fertilizer and plenty of it. When your corn begins to show its first tassels, give it a side dressing with nitrate of soda. Apply a heaping tablespoonful of the material for each corn plant, distributing it several inches from the corn and scuffing it into the soil with a light cultivation. Never cultivate corn, or any other crop, deeply. You may injure the roots. Another side dressing with nitrate of soda can be made when the first silks appear on the ears. If the soil is dry, irrigate so that the fertilizer will become available immediately.

Nobody ever loved sweet corn as much as corn worms do—first the budworms and then the earworms. Begin dusting with a multipurpose vegetable dust formulated for South Florida soon after your corn sprouts and keep it up on a five-day schedule until you see the first silks appear. Then dust every other day until the silks die. After that, return to the five-day schedule.

How many feet of rows do you allot for a corn patch? That depends on the size of your family and the number of your friends. Twenty feet of row will produce a great deal of corn for a small family. Remember that corn has to be harvested and eaten as soon as it is mature. Instead of planting all of your corn at one time, it's best to plant a succession of rows about three weeks apart.

Don't Forget the Roses

Plant your roses this month—the sooner after the first of November, the sooner you'll be picking flowers. If you followed the October calendar, you should have your beds all ready for planting now. If not, get them started immediately and you will still be able to enjoy a rose garden this winter.

Here are six good rules to follow in buying and growing roses:

1. Buy plants grafted on Dr. Huey, Cherokee, or Rosa fortunea stock. These are more resistant to soil and airborne diseases.

2. Plant in rich, well-drained soil and mulch heavily with peat or other organics.

3. Feed once a month.

4. Keep soil moist. Water container-grown roses daily and bed-grown plants every other day.

5. Apply disease and insect controls regularly; dust weekly.

When you set plants in beds, space them eighteen to twenty-four inches apart each way. Most tea roses will grow in southern Florida—some better than others—and with extra care hybrid teas can be grown year round. Easiest to grow are the florabundas, especially Floradora, Fashion, and Pinocchio. The climbers are less dependable, except for one, the yellow Marechal Niel. Avoid the novelty roses you see advertized for national markets—the type promoted as a "living fence," a "blue," or a "black" rose. Many of these oddities don't live up to their publicity anyway, even for northern gardeners.

Trust the Experience of Your Nurseryman

A shortcut to growing annuals in Florida is to buy your plants from nurserymen or from garden supply stores. These professionals grow the varieties they know from experience will thrive here, and you can lean on their advice.

Plant calendulas this month, and nasturtiums, petunias, phlox, and salvia. The planting calendar is wide open.

The mangos have been gone since September when the last of the Keitt and Brooks varieties were harvested, but the avocados begin coming in strong now. Booth 8's begin to mature after the first week in the month, and by the end of the month you can begin harvesting Booth 7's. For dooryard planting the Booth 7 is a very good tree. It is more resistant to diseases than the Booth 8, and the tree develops a good form. There's nothing more tropical than a well-grown Booth 7.

If you've had some chinch bugs in your Saint Augustine lawn during the summer and fall but not enough to kill the grass, don't be surprised if your lawn suddenly declines in November. Where the grass is badly damaged but not killed by these insects, it may decline badly during the dry season, first turning yellow in weak areas and then dying. If your lawn should begin to decline, start regular irrigations and apply some quickly available nitrogen. For quick results, apply Nu-Green at the rate of one and one-half pounds per 1,000 square feet or ammonium sulphate at the rate of five pounds per 1,000 square feet. Both can be dissolved in water and applied with a sprinkler can, if you like. Follow with a light irrigation if you use ammonium sulphate, since this material is not neutral in reaction and may burn your grass.

If in October you did not apply sulphur or another miticide for red spider, rust mites, and other members of the plant mite family, better get after that job in early November. Either apply a sulphur dust, lime-sulphur, or any of the several miticides such as Dimite or Aramite to mite-susceptible plants such as citrus, avocado, hibiscus, crotons, and ground covers. Sulphur dust is a practical remedy and easy to apply. It is a good idea to dust all of your favorite shrubs and vines with a sulphur dust once every two months during the dry winter season. Regular dusting may prevent mite-susceptible plants from shedding their leaves before the rainy season returns at the end of spring. For these plant mites, although they are so small that you must use a magnifying glass to see them, can do a

great deal of damage when they are permitted to accumu-
late on your plants in large numbers. The damage is often
done before you notice the presence of the mites. If you are
an inexperienced gardener, you may watch your plants shed
their rusty leaves without ever knowing the cause.

Two colorful bauhinias come into bloom this month: the
fall-flowering bauhinia, known to botanists as *Bauhinia
purpurea,* and Blake's bauhinia, known to botanists as
Bauhinia blakeana. The fall-flowering bauhinia is an oldtimer here. It is widely planted throughout South Florida.
Blake's bauhinia is a newcomer, introduced from Hong
Kong in 1952. Blake's bauhinia does not produce seeds. Its
origin is not known. Catholic monks, who found the tree
growing in China, took cuttings from the tree and grew
them. This bauhinia finally found its way to the botanical
garden in Hong Kong more than fifty years ago. A number
of attempts were made to introduce it to the Western
Hemisphere, but it was not until air transportation was
developed that an introduction was successful. Both the
Subtropical Experiment Station at Homestead and Fairchild
Tropical Garden introduced the tree independently at about
the same time. It is propagated only by air layering and by
budding. The very large flowers of Blake's bauhinia are
reddish purple, with much of the quality of a cattleya
orchid. *Bauhinia purpurea* is usually propagated from seeds.
The flowers vary in color from white to deep purple.

Many other common flowers begin to bloom in South
Florida before November is over. Flower buds on poinsettias begin to open, sprays of bloom begin to form on
bougainvillea vines, and many of the rare plants in the
Fairchild Tropical Garden begin to make a show of color.
By the middle of December there will be color everywhere,
for we will be well into the dry season, the time for bloom
in tropical Florida.

November Weather Calendar

Following are the average temperature, rainfall, and wind velocity figures for a normal. November in the Miami area.

Temperature. Average daily high: 79.9; average daily low: 69.4. Highest temperature ever recorded for the month: 90 in 1941; lowest temperature: 36 in 1914.

Rainfall. Average: 2.73 inches. Wettest November: 21.08 inches in 1952. Driest November: .23 of an inch in 1923.

Wind. Prevailing direction from the north. Average velocity: 9.2 miles an hour. On November 4, 1935, a hurricane wind of 94 miles an hour was recorded in Miami. Gusts reached 150 miles an hour.

Hurricanes. Little danger of hurricanes from now until next summer. Only one ever hit Miami in November.

Frost. While there's no record of frost in downtown Miami during November, frost has occurred in outlying residential and agricultural areas as early as November 20.

November Planting Calendar

Vegetables. Beans, beets, broccoli, Brussels sprouts, cabbage, carrots, cauliflower, celery, Chinese cabbage, collards, endive, garden peas, kohlrabi, leek, mustard, onion seeds and sets, parsley, peppers, pumpkins, radishes, rhubarb, romaine, rutabagas, spinach, squash, sweet corn, Swiss chard, tomatoes, and turnips.

Flowers. Asters, baby's breath, bachelor's buttons, balsam, calendulas, candytuft, carnations, cosmos, cockscomb, daisies, dianthus, forget-me-nots, gaillardia, globe amaranth, hollyhocks, lace flowers, lobelias, lupins, marigolds, nasturtiums, pansies, periwinkles, petunias, phlox, poppies, portulacas, salvia, scabiosa, snapdragons, statice, stock, strawflowers, sweet peas, sweet william, and verbenas.

Bulbs. Amaryllis, callas, gladiolus, lilies, narcissus, and zephyranthes.

November Garden Chores

Strawberries. Look out for pests attacking these plants. Begin dusting monthly with sulphur to keep down possible plant mite infestation.

Insects. Begin preventive measures for control of red spider mites and other smaller-than-the-eye-can-see pests that attack your ornamentals and fruit trees during the dry season. Begin monthly applications of sulphur dust or wettable sulphur to citrus, avocados, acalyphas, crotons, hibiscus, and other susceptible plants.

Tomatoes. Begin weekly spraying of tomato plants with a fungicide for control of late blight. Parzate, zineb, or manzate are good fungicides. The idea is to prevent late blight from hitting your plants. If you wait until you see blight lesions on the leaves, it may be too late to do any good.

Planting. Almost any annual or vegetable that you grew in your northern garden can be planted in South Florida this month. See the planting calendar.

Raspberries. Give tropical raspberries a final pruning this month and fertilize the plants if they need it. They should be in vigorous condition by the time flowering and fruiting begin late this winter.

DECEMBER

A Month of Color

By the time the first week of cool and pleasant December rolls around, your garden should be well underway; you are getting ready to cash in on your hours of labor during the previous months. If you haven't already done so, you'll soon be harvesting vegetables and cut flowers. The poinsettias are now coming into full bloom, and so are some of the bougainvilleas. Even the big clusters of fruit of the Christmas palm, the adonidia, are beginning to show color; and if luck is with you, yours will be masses of crimson before the end of the month. Of course, the citrus is beginning to turn orange or yellow, and the many colorful hibiscus blooms are still with us. If you have a Chinese hat plant (botanists call it holmskioldia), it will be full of brownish-red flowers this month. Also blooming in December is the Christmas vine (porana). This white flowering vine doesn't usually live up to its name in Florida, for it is usually through blooming by Christmas. December also is the flowering time for many of the finest orchids, which may be at their peak of color and form at Christmas.

December is usually a cool, dry month. The average rainfall for the month is under two inches while the average daily high temperature is about 76 degrees, with an average low of 60 degrees. This is an ideal climate, neither too hot nor too cold, with sunny days and billowy, rainless clouds breaking up the monotony of a blue sky. The evenings get chilly and sometimes downright cold. We do have occasional frosts in South Florida in December; during the month we've had some terrible freezes in middle Florida. The first of the two famous but disastrous freezes of the winter of 1894-1895 occurred in December. This freeze knocked all of the leaves off the citrus trees of North Florida, where most of the state's citrus groves were located. A second freeze in January, which came while the citrus trees were in new growth, was disastrous to Florida citrus growers. That freeze had a great deal of effect upon the history of Florida. It hastened the development of southeast Florida, for many growers moved down the east coast; and it eventually brought about the rapid development of central Florida, where the bulk of the citrus industry is now located.

Freezes Felt in Miami

Severe cold spells are rare in South Florida, but when they do come, they can take a severe toll on the unprepared gardener's plants. While it isn't by any means normal for hard freezes to hit South Florida, they should be regarded as a possibility. Gardeners who want to gamble with some of the ultratender exotic plants should not invest so much in them that their loss would kill their interest in tropical gardening.

Precautions May Be Worthwhile

Farmers and gardeners usually consider South Florida's frost period from November 20 to about the first of April. What does a South Florida gardener do when Jack Frost points an icy finger southward? Here are a few tips that you may want to learn if you will also remember that the same tips would bring you only grief in Pennsylvania or Maine during the winter:

1. Your garden is less susceptible to frost damage when the ground is wet than when it is dry. Therefore, when you hear that a frost is expected on the following morning, soak the ground thoroughly.

2. Young plants with mulch around them will freeze more quickly than when the soil about them is uncovered. Therefore, do not mulch tender young plants in winter. (Mulch prevents radiation of warmth from the soil and also collects dew, which freezes when the temperature drops to thirty-two degrees.)

3. Almost any kind of covering except metal will help to prevent plants from being injured by frost. Put the covering down before sundown of the evening before frost is forecast. Never use metal such as tin, since it is a conductor of cold.

4. Smudge pots not only help to prevent frost injury by raising the temperature, but the smoke acts as a cover for the plants. This smoke cover, by preventing loss of ground heat through radiation, may keep the air temperature about your plants as much as six degrees higher than the temperature in unprotected locations.

5. Frost damage may be prevented if you wash the frost off plants with a garden hose early in the morning soon after it forms. If the cold is severe enough for water to freeze, however, this practice is not recommended.

6. If you want to get a correct temperature reading during a cold spell, put your thermometer near the ground. A thermometer at eye level may register a temperature of thirty-five degrees while the temperature at ground level is thirty-two degrees, or freezing.

Small tender trees, such as year-old avocados or lychees,

can be covered with a bean hamper or a bushel basket. Young mango trees are susceptible to cold damage when the thermometer drops to thirty-two until they are four or five years of age. It's a good idea to bundle straw neatly about the trunks of small mango trees in November and let it remain until April.

Irrigate Thoroughly

Since December is a dry month, you will have to begin regular irrigation in order to keep your lawn a healthy green. How much watering is necessary and how often should water be applied? You can get all kinds of answers to this question. But the experts generally give the following advice.

Water periodically when the grass needs it; don't water just because you have a sprinkler system. Daily light sprinkling, dampening the grass and the top quarter-inch of the soil, is just about the worst thing you can do to your lawn. When you water, don't just sprinkle—water thoroughly, soaking the soil to a depth of several inches. Lay down the equivalent of an inch or more of water. And how can you tell when you've put down this much water? You can measure it by putting a pan underneath the sprinklers. One inch of water will moisten most soils to a depth of six inches.

When the soil is thoroughly wet, say to a depth of six inches, you don't need to water daily. You may not have to water more than once a week; in some locations watering every two or three weeks is enough. If you're in a high, sandy location, you may have to water more; in a lower place, you may need to water less.

By watering periodically and thoroughly you encourage deep rooting of your grass. If you sprinkle a little every day, keeping the top of the soil moist but leaving the soil dry underneath, you'll encourage the development of masses of roots near the surface. You will have what turfmen describe as shallow-rooted grass. Such a lawn cannot be neglected. Go off on a trip for a couple of weeks during the dry season and see what happens to your lawn—the roots will dry out and your grass will wither. Your lawn will be in plenty of trouble when you return unless you've been lucky enough for rains to save it while you were away. But deep-rooted grass may be neglected for weeks on end without suffering severe injury.

When you water periodically, you can do it at any time of the day. There's nothing to the theory that watering during the day will cause sunscald. How many pastures or fields of corn have you seen scalded after a midday shower?

Most Lawn Insects Are Inactive Now

You will not have to worry much about lawn insects during December, but the ordinary garden pests, such as caterpillars, cutworms, leafhoppers, and bug critters in general will be around all winter, competing with you for the harvest of flowers and vegetables. There will be a few pests on fruit trees and shrubs. One of the worst is red spider, a tiny fellow that ordinary eyes never see. Insect specialists list the red spider among the many kinds of plant mites, several of which compete for your better plants during the dry season. The mites are always worse during the dry season than during the rainy season. They are so small and helpless that they can't stay on plants that are periodically drenched by showers. By dusting every couple of months with sulphur, or better still, by spraying monthly with a miticide, you can keep these little fellows under control. Mites of one species or another are especially bad

Flower thrip, length: 1/15 inch

on crotons, hibiscus, acalyphas, avocados, and citrus.

Another wintertime pest is the thrip. All the various species of thrips are fairly easy to control with Sevin, Cygon systemic, and other insecticides such as Emo-Nik and Ortho Multi-Purpose Garden Spray. Weekly spraying is advised for gladioli to keep thrips from getting a head start.

The "red-banded" thrips, which often attack mangos, collect on the underside of the mango leaf, leaving a brown deposit. If not controlled, they can do so much damage to mango leaves that they are shed. They are most active near the ribs of the leaves. Spray the trees immediately after you see their signs and repeat the application in a week or ten days. Thrips often attack the new buds of hibiscus, causing them to drop.

Thrip, length: 1/20 inch

One of our rubber trees, *Ficus retusa,* is badly attacked by thrips, which twist the tips of the leaves and render the trees unsightly. These can also be controlled but most persons don't bother. One good way to prevent thrip damage to *Ficus nitida* is to buy one of the thrip-proof

Unless it is a "thrip-proof" variety, the giant ficus is subject to damage by this tiny insect

varieties. There is a variety of *Ficus nitida,* however, that thrips just don't damage. Maybe the leaves are not to their liking because they can't twist the tips into a safe place to live.

December, of course, is the time for Christmas trees— most of them spruce shipped in by the carload from the North. If you want to keep your Christmas tree green so that it won't start shedding its leaves before time to take it down, here's a tip: set it in a tub of moist soil or sand. The tree will soak up enough moisture to keep it green. Some people, whose trees have remained green over the holidays, plant them afterward in the hope that Florida's climate will keep them growing. These planted trees often send out new growth but will not put out roots. The leaves come from plant tissue and energy produced and stored during the previous summer.

Be Prepared for Mango Bloom

Mangos often come into bloom during December, although the unpredictable mango may bloom any time from November to March. Nevertheless, when the trees do come into bloom, it's time to get busy with fertilizer and with spray.

As soon as the bloom spikes elongate enough for you to be certain that your trees will bloom, give the trees a shot in the arm with a quickly available form of nitrogen. This is called the prebloom application. You can use a regular garden type of fertilizer, or you can use sulphate of ammonia. Since sulphate of ammonia is twenty percent nitrogen, five pounds contains a full pound of nitrogen. But it takes twenty-five pounds of a regular 6-6-6 fertilizer to provide a pound of nitrogen.

A tree ten to fifteen years of age with a spread of about twelve feet should receive about two pounds of sulphate of ammonia or ten pounds of 6-6-6. The application, which is made evenly under the entire canopy of the tree, should be followed by irrigation to make the nitrogen immediately available to the tree.

As soon as you can see the individual flowers forming, spray your trees with a fungicide as a fungus-disease preventive. Use neutral copper, bordeaux mixture, or one of the organic fungicides such as dithane, parzate, or manzate. Several additional applications of spray may be necessary, depending on weather conditions and also on how disease-free you want your fruit to be. A second fungicide application can be made as soon as the bloom panicles open well, and thereafter further treatments may be made about once a month.

December Weather Calendar

Following are the average temperature, rainfall, and wind velocity figures for a normal December in the Miami area.

Temperature. Average daily high: 76.6; average daily low: 59.7. Highest temperature ever recorded for the month: 85 in 1941 and 1968; lowest temperature: 30 in 1934.

Rainfall. Average: 1.73 inches. Wettest December: 9.03 inches in 1929. Driest December: .13 of an inch in 1968.

Wind. Prevailing direction from the north. Average velocity: 8.7 miles an hour. Highest wind velocity recorded in Miami during December: 65 miles an hour in 1940.

Frost. Protection advised all month.

Hurricane. There has never been a hurricane in Miami in December.

December Planting Calendar

Vegetables. Beans, beets, broccoli, Brussels sprouts, cabbage, carrots, cauliflower, celery, Chinese cabbage, collards, endive, garden peas, kohlrabi, leek, mustard, onion seeds and sets, parsley, peppers, pumpkins, radishes, rhubarb, romaine, rutabagas, spinach, squash, sweet corn, Swiss chard, tomatoes, and turnips.

Flowers. Asters, baby's breath, bachelor's buttons, balsam, calendulas, candytuft, carnations, cosmos, cockscomb, daisies, dianthus, forget-me-nots, gaillardias, globe amaranth, hollyhocks, lace flowers, lobelias, lupins, marigolds, nasturtiums, pansies, periwinkles, petunias, phlox, poppies, portulacas, salvia, scabiosa, snapdragons, statice, stock, strawflowers, sweet peas, sweet william, and verbenas.

Bulbs. Amaryllis, callas, dahlia tubers, Easter lilies, gladiolus, iris, narcissus, and zephyranthes.

December Garden Chores

Bulbs. Plant any varieties available in garden supply stores. Dahlia tubers are usually available this month.

Mangos. If these trees bloom this month, give them their prebloom fertilizer application. Apply a fertilizer when bloom panicles begin to elongate, when you know you are going to have a bloom. Irrigate to wash the fertilizer into the soil but keep water off the trees themselves.

Vegetables. Make progressive plantings of short crops this month. If you want late tomatoes, put in a seedbed before the end of the month.

Roses. Be sure to fertilize monthly and dust weekly with a special rose dust. Keep these plants growing richly and maintain their good health if you want an abundance of healthy bloom.

Bibliography

Books in Print

Craighead, Frank C. *Orchids and Other Air Plants of the Everglades National Park.* Coral Gables, Fla.: University of Miami Press, 1963.

Edson, Seton N. *Your Florida Garden Soils: 500 Questions and Answers.* Gainesville: University of Florida Press, 1963.

Fennell, T. A., Jr. *Orchids for Home and Garden.* New York: Holt, Rinehart and Winston, 1959.

Menninger, Edwin A. *Flowering Trees of the World.* New York: Hearthside Press, 1962.

Menninger, Edwin A. *Seaside Plants of the World.* New York: Hearthside Press, 1964.

Smiley, Nixon. *Tropical Planting and Gardening.* Coral Gables, Fla.: University of Miami Press, 1961.

Sturrock, David. *Fruits for Southern Florida.* Stuart, Florida: Southeastern Printing Company, 1959.

Watkins, John V. *Florida Landscape Plants.* Gainesville: University of Florida Press, 1969.

Watkins, John V., and Wolfe, Herbert S. *Your Florida Garden.* Fifth edition. Gainesville: University of Florida Press, 1968.

Watkins, John V. *Your Guide to Florida Landscape Plants; II: The*

Tropical Exotics. Gainesville: University of Florida Press, 1963.
Wilson, Bob and Catherine. *Bromeliads in Cultivation.* Miami: Hurricane House, 1963.

Available at Public Libraries

Barrett, Mary F. *Common Exotic Trees of South Florida.* Gainesville: University of Florida Press, 1956.
Chandler, William H. *Evergreen Orchards.* Philadelphia: Lea & Febiger: 1950.
Dorn, Mabel. *Tropical Gardening for South Florida.* South Miami: South Florida Publishing Company, 1952.
Dorn, Mabel. *Under the Coconuts in Florida.* South Miami: South Florida Publishing Company, 1949.
Fairchild, David. *The World Grows Round My Door.* New York: Charles Scribner's Sons, 1947.
Kuck, Loraine E., and Tongg, Richard C. *Hawaiian Flowers and Flowering Trees.* Rutland, Vermont: Charles E. Tuttle Company, 1958.
Kuck, Loraine E., and Tongg, Richard C. *The Modern Tropical Garden.* Honolulu: Tongg Publishing Company, Ltd., 1955.
MacMillan, H. F. *Tropical Planting and Gardening.* New York: The MacMillan Company, 1935.
Menninger, Edwin A. *What Flowering Tree is That?* Stuart, Florida: The Stuart Daily News, Inc., 1956.
Morton, Julia F., and Ledin, R. Bruce. *400 Plants of South Florida.* Coral Gables, Fla.: Text House, 1952.
Morton, Kendal and Julia. *Fifty Tropical Fruits of Nassau.* Coral Gables, Fla: Text House, 1946.
Smiley, Nixon. *Subtropical Gardening in Florida.* Coral Gables, Fla.: University of Miami Press, 1956.
West, Erdman, and Arnold, Lillian. *The Native Trees of Florida.* Gainesville: University of Florida Press, 1956.

Index

acalypha, 178
acerola, 41
acid-loving plants, 21
allamanda, 33
ammonium sulphate, 100
annuals, 33, 141-142
aphids, 29, 76, 142
ardisia, 42
avocado, 27, 98; air layering, 84; cold protection, 175; fertilizing, 154; mites, 178; pruning, 82; varieties, 96

babys breath, 142
bachelor's button, 142
bananas, 68
banyan, 42
Barbados cherry, 41
bauhinia, 58, 169; *Bauhinia variegata,* 58
bed preparation, 33
bees, 88
Big Cypress Swamp, 25, 161
birds, 40, 162-163
bischofia, 139

black-eyed susan, 142
black olives, 74
boron, 32
bottlebrush, 58
bougainvillea, 17, 58, 169; Crimson Lake, 77; fertilizing, 155-156; pruning, 82, 145; watering, 155-156
bucida, 74
budworm, 166
bulbs, 22, 62, 148, 181

calendula, 142
callistemon, 58
Caribbean Garden, 122
cassia, 17; *Cassia nodosa,* 77
caterpillar, 29, 88, 91, 156, 159
Ceylon peach, 104
chinch bug, 88, 91, 99, 117, 132, 144, 168
Chinese hat plant, 173
Chlorophytum somosum, 114
Christmas trees, 179
Christmas vine, 173
citrus, 27, 173-174; diseases, 29;

fertilizing, 29-30, 154; nutritional spray, 32-33; pests, 29, 56-57, 132, 147, 159, 178; planting, 29-30; pruning, 81
cockscomb, 142
cold protection, 175
copper, 29, 32-33, 69
county agricultural agent, 28
County Cooperative Extension Service, 28
crape myrtle, 77
croton, 78, 139, 178
cuphea, 86
cutworms, 159
cypress, 161
Cypress Gardens, 113, 122

Dade County Extension Service, 121
Dade County Parks Department, 58
dahlias, 142
day lily, 75
diseases, control, 21; prevention, 130, 141; transporting, 35
Dorn, Mabel, 10
duranta, 42
dynamite, 68
earworms, 166
Edison, Thomas Alva, 122
eugenia, 68
everglades, 138-139, 161
Everglades National Park, 26-27
Fairchild, Dr. David, 10
Fairchild Garden Association, 120
Fairchild Tropical Garden, 15, 60, 113, 120, 122, 124
ferns, 115
fertilizing, 19, 28, 31, 33, 36, 106, 117, 148, 150, 153, 159

Ficus nitida, 178-179; *F. retusa,* 139
fig, 117, rust, 133
Florida Cooperative Extension Service, 97, 120
Florida Nurserymen and Growers Association, 22
Florida State Department of Agriculture, 120
flowers, annuals, 33
foot rot, of citrus, 29
frost, 57, 175
fruit trees, 94; fertilizing, 28, 95
fumigation, 141, 151
fungus, 76, 101, 106, 109, 133

gaillardia, 142
gardenia, 21; *Gardenia thunbergia,* 66
gardening; bed preparation, 33; fundamentals, 18; planting, 76, pushing growth, 19
Gifford, Dr. John C., 10
golden shower tree, 77
governor's plum, 42
grapefruit, 27, 96
grass, Bahia, 154; Bermuda, 73-74, 98-99, 101; centipede, 16, 34, 99, 147, 154-155, chinch bugs, 99, 117; rye, 154-155; St. Augustine, 16, 99-101, 117, 144, 154; zoysia, 16, 99, 100-101, 154-155
grasshoppers, 29, 76, 88
greasy spot, on citrus, 29
ground covers, 85, 113
guava, 33, 42, 140
gumbo limbo, 68
gummosis, 29

hammocks, 68

herbicides, 71
herbs, 146, 159
hibiscus, fertilizing, 33; flowering; 139-140; location, 20-21; pruning, 82
holmskioldia, 173
house plants, 117
humus, 32, 69
hurricanes, 80, 104, 136-137, 157, 173, 178

insecticides, 88, 156
insects, 101, 141, 143, 165, 171
iron, 32-34, 69
iron sulphate, 99
ixoras, 20, 33, 140

jacaranda, 75
jambolan plum, 139
Japanese beetle, 90
Japanese Garden, 123

kalanchoe, 86, 115
katydids, 86

ladybug, 88
lagerstroemia, 140; *Lagerstroemia speciosa,* 77
lancewood, 68
landclearing, 68
land crabs, 147
landscaping, 64-75, 108-113
lawns, 51, 71; fertilizing, 133, 148, 159; insects, 105, 146, 177; mowing, 115-116; top-dressing, 87-88, 91; varieties of grass, 98; watering 175-177; weed killers, 71-73
leafhoppers, 76, 165
leaf miners, 164
leaf rollers, 142

Leucophyllum texanum, 139
lily, day, 75
lime, 33
limestone, 59, 67, 69-70, 125
lime tree 96; key, 29-30; Persian, 27, 30
liriope, 115
lychee, 33, 97, 154, 175
lysiloma, 42, *Lysiloma bahamensis,* 110

McKee's Jungle, Gardens, 113, 122
magnesium, 29
mahogany, 74
malathion, 142
Malpighia glabra, 41
manganese, 32-33, 69
mango, fertilizing, 28, 117, 154, 180-181; flavor, 104; protection from cold, 176; pruning, 82; ripening, 140, 167-168; spraying, 179; varieties, 96
maple, red, 161; Southern, 25
marigold, 142
marl, 87
mastic, 68
Matheson Hammock, 124
mealy bug, 148
melaleuca, 139
melanose, 29
Menninger, Edwin A., 16
Mexican sunflower, 142
Miami Beach Conservatory, 123
mildew, 106
mites, 36, 62, 51
miticide, 21, 132, 144
mole cricket, 159, 165
muck, 87
mulch, 32, 57, 59, 69, 175
muntinga, 42

nasturtium, 142
native plants, 16
nematodes, 57, 115
neutral metals, 33
nitrogen, 31, 100
nutritional deficiencies, 69
nutritional sprays, 36

oak, 42, 68
Okinawan hawthorne, 60
oolite, 69
oranges, 27, 29, 96; Temple, 96
Orchid Jungle, 124
orchids, Christmas-flowering,
    173; mites on, 132; repotting,
    101-102, 106
osmunda fern, 101
oyster plant, 114

palms, 124; adonidia, 124, 130,
    173; Alexander, 124; betel
    nut, 125; cabbage, 125, 129;
    Christmas, 173; *Dictyosperma
    album*, 130; coconut, 20, 110,
    129, 139; *Cocos plumosa*,
    130; *Cocothrinax wrightii*,
    125; Colombian wax, 125;
    Cuban belly, 125; *Dictyo-
    sperma album*, 130; fishtail,
    126; landscaping, 129-130;
    hurricane, 130; royal, 20;
    sabal, 125; silver, 68; sugar,
    126, 129; thrinax, 126; *Tri-
    thrinax brasiliensis*, 126
papayas, 36, 139; fertilizing, 148
Parrot Jungle, 113
peat moss, 115
Peltophorum inerme, 77
peperomia, 86, 115
periwinkle, 86, 142
Perrine, Dr. Henry, 9
philodendron, 114

phosphate, 31
pineapples, 68
pines, 20, 70-71; Caribbean, 68
planting, 76, 151, 171
poincianas, 17, 74; dwarf, 140;
    yellow, 77
poinsettias, 51, 55, 145, 147,
    159, 164, 173; pruning, 56, 82
pole beans, 54, 165
pongam, 74
porana, 173
portulaca, 16
potash, 31
potato, 40
pot holes, 68
pothos, 114
propagation, 62, 86; air layering,
    84, 148; cuttings, 51, 66-67,
    85
pruning, 20, 56, 77-79, 81, 91,
    105, 133, 145, 148, 159; root,
    65-66
Purple Queen, 114, 123
pushing growth, 19

queen's crape myrtle, 77
quick-decline, of citrus, 29

radish, 164
rain, 137-139
Raphiolepis indica, 60
raspberry, 171
Redland Fruit and Spice Park,
    123
red maple, 161
red spider mite, 102
Rhoeo spathacea, 114
rose, 35; culture, 166-167; dust-
    ing, 35, 131; leaf spot, 131;
    location, 20; preparing beds,
    147, 152-153; spraying, 131
rubber tree, 139

rust, 133
rust mites, 168

sacred fig, 74
sand, 91
sapodilla, 33
Sarasota Jungle Gardens, 113
scale, 21, 102, 106, 143
scrub willow, 161
seed catalogs, 22, 53
seedlings, 141-142
Seteresia tampiciana, 114
severenia, 42
Sevin, 143
silver trumpet tree, 58
Simpson Park, 124
Simpson, Professor Charles
   Torrey, 10
slug, 106, 143-144
Small, Dr. John K., 9
smudge pot, 175
snail, 143
sod webworm, 99, 101, 142
soil preparation, 19, 86, 151
sooty mold, 29, 143
Southern maple, 25
sterilizing soil, 141
stock, 142
strangler fig, 68
strawberry, 152, 159, 171
sulphur, 21, 35, 51, 88, 168, 177;
   sulphur-zineb, 115
sunflower, Mexican, 142
Sunken Garden, 113
sweet corn, 165-166

Tabebuia argentea, 58; *T. pallida,*
   77
tamarind, 110
tangelo, 29, 96

tangerine, 27, 29, 96
tetrazygia, 68
Texas silverleaf, 139
tomato, 40, 132, 164, 171
tomato hornworm, 142
torenia, 142
tradescantia, 85
tristeza, 29

United States Army Corps of
   Engineers, 26
United States Department of
   Agriculture, Plant Introduction Station, 15
University of Florida, 29; Agricultural Experiment Station,
   121; herbarium, 121; Subtropical Experiment Station, 15,
   121

vegetables, 33, 76, 141-142, 181;
   industry, 17

wasp, 88
watering, 19, 34, 51, 57, 101,
   176-177
watermelons, 40
wedelia, 85, 115
weed killer, 71-73
West Indian cherry, 33, 41, 104
whitefly, 29, 133
woman's tongue tree, 74
woolly caterpillar, 143

yellow elder, 140

Zebrina pendula, 114
zinc, 29, 32-33
zinnia, 142